D1301089

OTHER TITLES OF INTEREST FROM ST. LUCIE PRESS

Creating Quality in the Classroom

New Schools for a New Century:
  A Leader's Guide to High School Reform

Quality in Education: An Implementation Handbook

Teams in Education: Creating an Integrated Approach

Total Quality in Higher Education

The Baldrige Award for Education:
  How to Measure and Document Quality Improvement

Continuous Improvement in Education Video Series
  • Adopting the New Education Paradigm
  • Out of Theory Into Practice
  • Using Quality to Improve Administrative and Student Outcomes

Quality Improvement Handbook

Improving Service Quality:
  Achieving High Performance in the Public and Private Sectors

Total Quality Management: Text, Cases and Readings, 2nd Edition

For more information about these titles call, fax or write:

St. Lucie Press
100 E. Linton Blvd., Suite 403B
Delray Beach, FL 33483
TEL (407) 274-9906 • FAX (407) 274-9927

$S\overset{t}{L}$

Quality in
EDUCATION
An Implementation
HANDBOOK

Quality in
EDUCATION
An Implementation
HANDBOOK

Jerome S. Arcaro

S^t_L

St. Lucie Press
Delray Beach, Florida

Printed and bound in the U.S.A. Printed on acid-free paper.
10   9   8   7   6   5   4   3   2   1

Library of Congress Cataloging-in-Publication Data

Arcaro, Jerome S.
    Quality in education: an implementation handbook / by Jerome S. Arcaro
        p.   cm.
    Includes index.
    ISBN 1-884015-58-1
    1. School management and organization—United States—Handbooks, manuals, etc. 2. Total quality management—United States—Handbooks, manuals, etc. 3. School improvement programs—United States—Handbooks, manuals, etc . I. Title.
LB2805.A6   1995
371′.00973—dc20   94-46378
                                                                                        CIP

Phone: (407) 274-9906
Fax: (407) 274-9927

S$\overset{t}{\text{L}}$

Published by
St. Lucie Press
100 E. Linton Blvd., Suite 403B
Delray Beach, FL 33483

TABLE OF CONTENTS

PREFACE

Quality in Education: An Implementation Handbook is designed to help education professionals implement the principles of quality in their school or district. During the past 25 years, more than 250 school improvement programs have been implemented in the United States. Very few, if any, of these programs have been successful. Effective reform in education requires the participation of all the stakeholders. Education must be viewed as an integrated system within society rather than a separate organization that is a supplier to society. Dr. W. Edwards Deming's Total Quality Management philosophy addresses these key issues. Unfortunately, they were overlooked by many of the previous educational reform programs.

Quality works in education as well as in business. It is a revolution. However, quality takes time, perseverance, a change in attitude by all, and an investment in training for every staff member. Many education leaders fail in their attempts to implement quality because they are unwilling to make the commitment necessary for success. Many education professionals also expect quality to be the "fast-food approach" to solving today's complex educational problems.

Through the use of this handbook, you will learn the importance of establishing a shared definition of quality within your school or district. A successful quality program develops a common vision among administrators, staff, teachers, students, parents, business, government, and the community. New techniques that you can use to manage change within your organization are discussed throughout this book. The examples presented demonstrate how TQM can be applied to every educational process, from managing classroom functions to building maintenance.

This handbook will enable you to begin to change the way people in your district or school view education and their work. The tools and techniques discussed provide the foundation that you will need to develop a quality culture. You are embarking on a quality journey that will last for the rest of your life. It is extremely important that you understand the basic concepts and tools of quality before you begin your journey. Success *demands* that you build a strong quality foundation. This book provides the knowledge, tools, and techniques that you will need to begin your journey.

ABOUT THE AUTHOR

Jerome S. Arcaro is President of Galileo Quality Institute. As one of Galileo's key instructors, he has had extensive experience in implementing Total Quality Management in education and in helping schools implement quality programs.

Mr. Arcaro was first introduced to the concepts of quality in 1978 while employed at the New Hampshire State Prison in Concord. He was in charge of developing a computer-based education program to provide participants with the skills needed to gain meaningful employment upon their return to society. The major challenge faced by Mr. Arcaro was getting the students to make an investment in their future. Personal investment was viewed as the key factor in the success of the program.

The prison's computer educational program was founded upon the principles of quality. The curriculum was based on total student involvement. The students developed a structure that helped them cope with institutional pressures. The program was a total success. Within the first year of the program, the inmates created a new prison industry. Disciplinary problems for inmates participating in the program declined, and the inmates worked a longer and more demanding work schedule than the rest of the prison population. The inmates made a personal commitment to the success of the program. On a return visit to the Department of Correction in 1994, Mr. Arcaro was told that the program continued to be a success. Unlike other institutional education programs, this program withstood the test of time. It has now become institutionalized.

Mr. Arcaro developed the "Excellence in Education Management System"™, which is currently being implemented in over 500 schools in the United States and Europe. For the past four years, he has been developing and implementing quality-based programs in schools in America and England. Mr. Arcaro provides quality training programs for education professionals and is a frequent guest speaker at quality forums.

HINTS FOR SUCCESS

Throughout this book, the use of videos and exercises will be recommended to facilitate your learning experience. These tools reinforce the concepts being discussed and help you to effectively apply the ideas in your organization. As you learn the quality methodology, you should discuss your experiences with other members of your district or school. This will enable everyone to benefit from your learning experience.

Every quality program includes four essential components. First, there must be a commitment to change, and school board members and administrators must demonstrate their commitment to change. Quality is change, and the thought of change evokes fear in many people. Your commitment to change will help to alleviate the fears of the people in your district or school.

One of our early experiences in implementing quality in education was in Soundwell College, Bristol, England. Mr. David Ekinsmyth had recently been appointed principal when the school decided to embark on quality. Unfortunately, the English economy went into a deep recession shortly after the school began to implement quality. The poor economy forced the central government to make drastic changes in the way education was funded. One of the major policies adopted by the central government forced every college in England to become a private corporation. The transformation from a public institution to a private corporation was a major culture shock for everyone at Soundwell College. The college has since achieved corporate status and is using the quality philosophy to gain a competitive advantage in a very competitive market environment.

Remember, not everything is going to go right the first time or every time. Mr. Ekinsmyth encountered many obstacles before he encountered success. You must be prepared to allow people to fail. It is okay to fail if we learn from our failures.

Second, you must have a clear understanding of where your school or district is today. Unfortunately, many of the previous attempts to improve the quality of education failed because this issue was overlooked. Efforts to solve the problem began before the problem had been clearly identified. Before you can make any successful and lasting change, you must know how the systems are working today.

Third, you must have a clear vision for the future, and everyone in the school or district must "buy into" your vision. The vision is a beacon that guides your team on its quality journey. Every quality program will experience difficulties. Your vision will help people to remain focused and committed to the quality transformation.

Finally, you must have a plan for implementing quality in your district or school. Your plan should provide your team with a set of guidelines which govern the implementation process. Your quality plan must be a living document. Both the internal and external environmental factors that impact education will change. Your plan must constantly be updated to reflect these changes. No quality program is stagnant and no two programs are identical. Your quality program must reflect your educational environment.

This handbook is intended to help you gain insight into how you are currently thinking and behaving in relation to quality. You will learn how to use the tools and techniques of quality to improve the way you work. By sharing your educational experience with other members of your staff, you will begin to build a quality vision for your district or school.

CHAPTER 1

INTRODUCTION

Quality is the single most important issue in education, business, and government today. We all recognize that there are problems with today's education system. Students are leaving or graduating from high school and college unprepared to meet the demands of society. This problem has a ripple effect throughout society. Students who are not prepared to become responsible, productive citizens become a burden to society. These students, products of an education system that does not focus on quality, increase social welfare costs. They impact the criminal justice system, they are not prepared to meet the needs of the next generations, and, most important, they are citizens who feel alienated from society.

If the quality of education is to improve, however, the improvement must be led by today's education professionals. Quality management is a vehicle that education professionals can use to cope with the "forces of change" that are buffeting our nation's education system. The knowledge needed to improve our education system already exists within the education community. The major difficulty education professionals face today is their inability to deal with the "system failures" that are preventing them from developing or implementing new educational processes that will improve the quality of education.

Education must undergo a paradigm shift. Old norms and beliefs must be challenged. Schools must learn to work with fewer resources. Education professionals must help students develop the skills they need to compete in a global economy. Unfortunately, the attitude in many schools is that the quality of education will improve only when society provides education with more money. Money is not the key to improving the quality of education. The quality of education will improve when administrators, teachers, staff, and school board members develop new attitudes that focus on leadership, teamwork, cooperation, accountability, and recognition.

During the four years that we have been implementing quality in education, we have encountered only one experience of failure. The district was a member of a nation-wide school improvement program. Prior to our becoming involved with the district, we completed an environmental assessment. The data collected indicated that the school improvement effort was failing; there was a low level of trust within the district, and the district lacked a commitment to change. In hindsight, the data supported our staff's recommendation to walk away from any involvement with the district. However, we committed our efforts to the program.

The district was looking for a "quick fix." During the previous three summers, the superintendent had hired consultants to work with the staff to improve the results of the school improvement program. Every consultant experienced failure. The lack of commitment to change was clearly demonstrated by the superintendent at a school board workshop.

I advised the superintendent that the training should begin by 7:00 p.m. and that it should last for no more than two hours. The workshop was scheduled to begin at the conclusion of a school board meeting. At the meeting during which the workshop was scheduled, the superintendent added a very controversial item to the agenda. The meeting did not conclude until 9:45 p.m., and the attitude of many members of the board was not conducive to training at that point. They wanted to go home. Rather than postpone the session, I reduced the focus of the training. This was a mistake on my part. As you can imagine, the session was a failure and the program was terminated. You can guess who was blamed for the failure.

Dr. Jon Whan, superintendent of schools for the Bay-Arenac Intermediate School District, is one of the progressive quality leaders in education. We have been working with the Bay-Arenac Intermediate School

District for the past two years. During the initial year of the project, we focused on helping the staff develop a quality culture. Every staff member was provided with the opportunity to participate in quality training programs; staff were trained as quality facilitators. The district adopted vision and mission statements, and staff clearly identified the district's critical success factors. Individual and departmental quality goals and objectives were adopted to ensure the district's success. Whenever the personal or department goals conflicted with the district's quality goals, Dr. Whan met with the staff to resolve the conflict.

Dr. Whan clearly "walks the talk." He is committed to quality. He does not always agree with the suggestions and recommendations of the staff, but he always listens to them. The quality methodology is being used by Dr. Whan to encourage the staff to find new ways to improve efficiency, productivity, and service quality. The staff is using new processes to develop budgets, resolve problems, and develop new programs. The district is succeeding in Michigan's new educational environment.

WHAT DOES IT TAKE FOR A SCHOOL OR DISTRICT TO BE SUCCESSFUL?

Many of today's education professionals lack the knowledge or expertise necessary to prepare students for entry into a global labor market. Tradition prevents many educational processes from being changed to meet student needs. Society is demanding that the quality of education improve, but society fails to support education's efforts to improve. Many of our nation's education professionals are fearful of change and do not know how to cope with the new requirements expected of them.

Education professionals must be aware of the fact that a commercial quality program will not work in education. The culture, environment, and work processes are different in each organization. Education professionals must be provided with a program that is specifically designed for education. One of the key components of a quality program for education is the development of a measurement system that enables education professionals to document and demonstrate the added value of education for the students and the community. As will be discussed later in this book, we have customized the Malcolm Baldrige National Quality Award criteria for education.

Additionally, society and education must eliminate their short-term focus. The modern world is one in which the only constant is change. Change is a precarious matter. Quality management can help schools cope with change in a positive and constructive manner. A quick fix will not solve today's problems in education. That has been tried in the past and has failed. It will take dedication, focus, and a constancy of purpose to improve the quality of education. To achieve a quality education environment, all of the stakeholders of education must be committed to the transformation process.

HISTORY OF QUALITY

Dr. W. Edwards Deming is generally recognized as the "father of quality." Dr. Deming received his Ph.D. in mathematics and physics from Yale University. He was first introduced to the basic tenets of traditional management principles in the late 1920s, as a summer employee at Western Electric's famous Hawthorne plant in Chicago. This experience led him to ask, "How can firms best motivate their employees?" Deming found the traditional motivation system in use at the time to be degrading and economically unproductive. Under that system, work incentives were linked to piecework to maximize worker output, followed by an inspection process in which defective items were subtracted from the worker's piecework credits.

During the 1930s, Deming collaborated with Walter A. Shewhart, a statistician working at Bell Telephone Laboratories, to develop statistical control techniques that could be applied to management processes. Deming recognized that a statistically controlled management process gave the manager a newfound capacity to systematically determine when to intervene and, equally important, when to leave a process alone. During World War II, Deming got his first opportunity to demonstrate to the government how Shewhart's statistical quality control methods could be taught to workers and put into practice in our nation's busy war plants.

At the conclusion of World War II, Deming left government service and set up a private consulting practice. The State Department, one of his early clients, sent Deming to Japan in 1947 to help prepare a national census in that country. American managers soon forgot their wartime quality control lessons and returned to their prewar love affair with traditional management practices. However, Deming's evolving quality control methods received a warm reception in Japan. The Japanese attribute their economic success to Dr. Deming's quality methodology.

Deming's philosophy is prone to put quality in human terms. When a firm's work force is committed to doing a good job and has a solid managerial process in which to act, quality will flow naturally. A more practical, composite definition of quality might read: Quality is a predictable degree of variation for adopted standards and dependability at low cost. Quality is customer driven and market focused. The methodological core of Deming's quality management approach is the use of simple statistical techniques to continuously improve output. Only through statistical verification can the manager know that he or she has a problem and find the causes of the problem.

Some of Deming's key principles as applied to education are:

- School board members and administrators must make the pursuit of quality an educational goal.

- Emphasis should be placed on preventing students from failing instead of detecting failure after the fact.

- The use of statistical control methods, if rigorously applied, can help to improve administrative and student outcomes.

Dr. Joseph M. Juran is also recognized as one of the "fathers of quality." Dr. Juran received his education in engineering and law. Like Deming, Juran is a distinguished statistician. Juran defines quality as "fitness for use" and maintains that the basic quality mission of a school is "to develop programs and services that meet the needs of the user, i.e., students and society." Furthermore, Juran states that "fitness for use" is properly determined from the viewpoint of the user as opposed to the provider.

Juran's quality outlook reflects a rational, matter-of-fact approach to business organization and is heavily dependent on sophisticated "shop floor" planning and quality control processes. The focal point of his quality management philosophy is the organization's belief in the productivity of the individual. Quality is ensured by making sure that each individual has the building blocks necessary to do his or her job properly. With the proper tools, workers will produce products and services that consistently meet customer expectations.

Like Deming, Juran also played a significant role in rebuilding Japan after World War II. He was recognized by the Japanese for the development of quality control in Japan and the facilitation of a friendship between the United States and Japan. His search for the underlying principles of the management process led to his focus on quality as the ultimate goal.

Some of Juran's points include:

- The pursuit of quality is a never-ending process.

- Quality improvement is an ongoing process, not a one-shot program.

- Quality requires hands-on leadership by school board members and administrators.

- Massive training is a prerequisite of quality.

- Everyone in a school must be trained.

If the teachings of Deming and Juran seem familiar, they should. Much of their thinking has been both adopted and adapted by many organizations in America. The point is that the establishment of quality as the basic educational principle for schools is grounded in the proven track record and results that others have achieved with similar philosophies and strategies.

Juran predicted the success of the Japanese in 1966 in a speech to the European Organization for Quality Control. He said:

> The Japanese are headed for world quality leadership and will attain it in the next two decades because no one else is moving toward it at the same pace.

TOTAL QUALITY SCHOOLS

If implemented properly, Total Quality Management (TQM) is a methodology that can help education professionals cope with today's changing environment. It can be used to alleviate fear and increase trust in schools. TQM can be used as a tool to establish an alliance between education, business, and government. Educational alliances ensure that the school or district's education professionals are provided with the resources necessary to develop quality education programs. TQM can provide the focus for education and society. It establishes a flexible infrastructure that can quickly respond to society's changing demands. It helps education to cope with budget and time constraints. *Total Quality Management makes it easier to manage change.*

The transformation to a Total Quality School begins with the adoption of a shared dedication to quality by the school board, administration, staff, students, parents, and the community. The process begins with the development of a quality vision and mission for the district and for each school and department within the district. The quality vision focuses on meeting the needs of the customers, providing for total community involvement in the program, developing systems to measure the added value of education, support systems that the staff and students need to manage change, and continuous improvement, always striving to make the products of education better.

Customer Focus

In order for schools to develop a quality focus, everyone in the school system must recognize that every educational output has customers. In a recent survey of 150 superintendents of schools to measure their understanding of quality, sadly 35% of the respondents surveyed indicated that they do not believe that schools have customers. Unless everyone in the education community recognizes the fact that there are customers for every educational output, the quality of education cannot be improved.

Total Involvement

Everyone must be involved in the quality transformation. Management must be committed to focusing on quality. As indicated by the program presented in this book, the school and district administrative management teams must work to provide the staff and students with the support they need to change the way they do their work today. Without this commitment, the quality program cannot succeed.

The quality transformation begins with the adoption of a new education paradigm. The old ways of working and thinking must be discarded. In education, it is extremely difficult for people to develop a new education paradigm. Two major beliefs in education block any attempt to create a quality education system. First, many education professionals believe that the quality of education is dependent upon the amount of money allocated to education. The more money invested in education, the higher the quality of education. Recent case studies dispel this belief.

A recent editorial in the *New Hampshire Union Leader* identified several examples where spending for education far exceeded the rate of inflation. Furthermore, the editor stated that the quality of education in these examples did benefit from the increase in spending. Over the past decade, the state of Connecticut has invested millions of dollars in its education system. Connecticut's per student expenditures are among the highest in the nation. Teachers and administrators are also among the highest paid and the student–teacher ratio is among the lowest in the nation. However, Connecticut has not realized any significant improvement in the quality of education. The state is being asked to invest more money in education systems.

Furthermore, many education professionals still view education as a "good old boy network." They resist any attempt on the part of non-education professionals to influence system changes. Many education professionals publicly state that they are committed to Dr. Deming's quality transformation. However, their actions indicate that they have not developed a new philosophy of education based upon Dr. Deming's Fourteen Points of quality. Until these two major issues are addressed, the quality of education will not significantly improve in America.

Measurement

This is an area where schools often fail. Traditionally, schools measure the quality of their output by student achievement. The basic measures of student output are test scores. If test scores are improving, obviously the quality of education must be improving. Education professionals must learn to measure quality. They need to understand the data collection and analysis requirements of the process under review. Once they learn to collect and analyze data, education professionals can measure and demonstrate the added value of education.

Systems View of Education

Education must be viewed as a system. This is the most difficult concept for education professionals to understand. Generally, people in education begin to improve the system without developing a full understanding of how the system operates. In a recent detailed analysis of a college in England, it was surprising to find that the college had not documented a single process or procedure. Functions were performed because they had always been performed. Only by viewing education as a system can education professionals eliminate waste from education and improve the quality of every educational process.

Continuous Improvement

The basic concept of quality is that everything can be improved. According to the old management philosophy, "If it isn't broke, don't fix it." Quality is based on the concept that every process can be improved and that no process is perfect. According to the new management philosophy, "If it isn't broke, improve it, because if you don't, someone else will." This is the concept of continuous improvement.

TOTAL QUALITY SCHOOLS MODEL

As depicted in the model on the next page, the criteria for a Total Quality School are labeled "the pillars of quality" for education. They are essential ingredients for every successful quality initiative. The pillars of quality are universal. They can be applied to every organization in education, from classroom activities to building maintenance. All the pillars are of equal importance. You cannot attain Total Quality School status unless all of the pillars are present in your education system. However, the most important component of quality is the foundation upon which the quality program is built. The school or district's beliefs and values will determine the strength and success of the quality transformation. The school or district must develop a strong quality foundation based on the personal beliefs and values of the people working in the system.

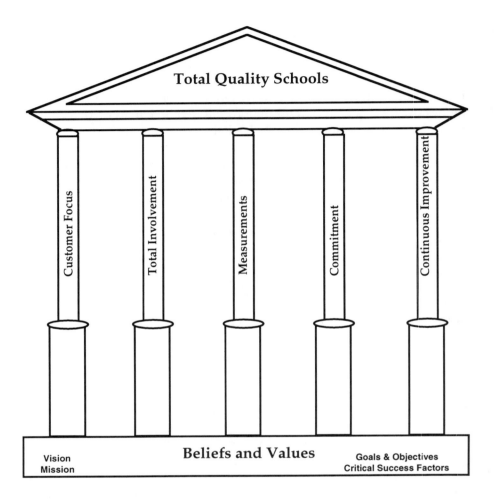

Quality must come to mean as much to school board members and administrators as it does to students and staff. The school board must create a new education paradigm for the community. Education must be valued for the contribution it makes to developing students as valued citizens who are better prepared to meet future academic and business challenges. A Total Quality School creates an environment that enables everyone to bring measurable quality improvements to their work processes.

The "pillars of quality" provide the staff with the focus and direction that is necessary for any quality initiative. They enable the staff to measure and document the added value of the quality initiative to the students and society. Focus cannot be limited to just one pillar. To develop a district-wide or school-wide quality culture, you must focus on all of the pillars at the same time.

CHAPTER 2

LEADERSHIP

The *New World Dictionary* defines a leader as "a person or thing that leads; directing, commanding, or guiding head, as of a group or activity." This definition will not work in today's quality-conscious environment. A **quality leader** is defined as a person who measures his or her success by the success of the individuals within the organization. The Quality Leadership Pyramid depicts the changing roles of today's education professionals.

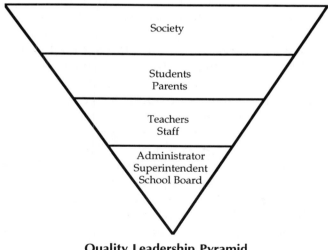

Quality Leadership Pyramid

The role of the school board, superintendent, and administrators is to provide the focus and direction for the district and schools. They have the vision for the future, and they have the ability to get the teachers and staff to accept ownership of the vision as their own. This is referred to as **shared responsibility**. The teachers and staff are committed to achieving the vision.

When this model is presented, many people often challenge the position that the school board, superintendent, and administrators have the vision for the district and schools. They argue that the vision should be created by everyone rather than just upper management. In the real world, the vision for any education system is created by the school board and superintendent with input from the community and staff. The quality leader in education has the ability to draw the vision from the rest of the staff in the district or school and inspire the staff to take the steps necessary to achieve the vision. Expanding on our first definition, this is the concept of **shared responsibility and empowerment**.

School boards and administrators do not like the word "empowerment." Empowerment does not mean that everyone will be creative and do whatever they want to do. Empowerment means that people are encouraged to be open, creative, and innovative in finding new ways of working to achieve their vision. Shared responsibility and empowerment means that people are encouraged to be open, creative, and innovative in finding new ways to work within the system that enable everyone to achieve the system-wide vision. This definition means that people recognize the interdependence that exists between people and functions. The enlightened quality leader motivates the staff to achieve the ultimate goal of the organization—**continuous quality improvement**.

In the Quality Leadership Pyramid, the school board, superintendent, and administrators must provide the staff and teachers with the resources they will need to succeed. This means that the absolute power once held by the school board, superintendent, and administrators is no longer allowed to exist. The words *authority* and *power* are removed from the vocabulary of a quality leader. This does not mean, however, that the school board, superintendent, and administrators do not have to make the decisions imposed upon them by law, policy, or government regulations. When the school board, superintendent, and administrators are required to make these decisions, the decisions reflect the concerns, opinions, attitudes, and interests of all the staff and customers.

What is the role of the teacher and staff in the Quality Leadership Pyramid? The major complaint from administrators today is that teachers and staff do not make decisions even when they are provided with the opportunity to do so. In the Quality Leadership Pyramid, everyone is a leader. To achieve the quality vision for education, the teacher must get the students to assume ownership for the vision and must be willing to listen to and act on the creative and innovative ideas the students have for achieving the vision. The teacher must give up the "absolute" authority in the classroom.

During the development of a computer-based education program to provide inmates at the New Hampshire State Prison with the skills needed to gain meaningful employment upon their return to society, the students were asked to define a quality classroom. They described a classroom that provided for more individual freedom and accountability. The students wanted to define a classroom environment that included the enforcement of the prison's rules of conduct. When the concept was presented to the warden, his first reaction was that it could never work in a prison environment. However, he reluctantly agreed to implement the process.

Shortly after the process was implemented, an incident occurred that could have destroyed this initiative. Someone took some items from one of the classrooms. The incident was investigated by the security force, and it was determined that one of the inmates in the program was responsible for removing the articles. The inmates were reminded of the new procedures in effect in the program and asked the person who took the items to return them to the classroom after lunch. The person who took the items returned them to the classroom and then turned himself in to security. The incident was resolved in a positive manner, and there was no disruption to the classroom environment. In the past, this would have become a major incident for the teacher and the administration.

As a quality leader, everyone is responsible for removing the obstacles that prevent high performance. The vision provides people with the direction to follow. Once the direction is known, the next step is to remove the obstacles and barriers that prevent people from achieving excellence in their performance. Everyone wants to be a high performer. A quality leader removes the obstacles that prevent people from being high performers.

The major challenge for quality education leaders is to remove the organizational barriers that prevent people from succeeding. Today's education systems reinforce the "this too shall pass" mentality. For example, one barrier that prevents schools from improving the quality of education is the grading system. Grades are used to measure the students' progress in learning. However, grades cannot measure the students' knowledge and use of the subject matter. In addition, some teachers have actually implemented the practice of giving students a "prep test" to ensure higher scores on the actual test. Society demands that we keep the grading system, and nothing ever changes.

Today's education structures are being challenged from all sides. The state of Michigan has changed its funding formulas for education. In many instances, school are not receiving as much money as they once did. Ohio and New Hampshire are fighting community-initiated lawsuits over the way education is funded. Communities are contracting with private organization for the management of their education systems. Quality leaders in education are sorely needed, and that need will not disappear. Yet education professionals continue to do what they have done in the past and continue to achieve the results of the past— poor student performance. The crisis in education is drawing nearer. If today's education professionals do not change their leadership styles, a major crisis will occur, from which recovery for the education system as we know it today may be difficult or even impossible.

CHAPTER 3

MALCOLM BALDRIGE NATIONAL QUALITY AWARD FOR EDUCATION

This award is named for Malcolm Baldrige, who served as secretary of commerce from 1981 until his tragic death in a rodeo accident in 1987. President Ronald Reagan appointed Mr. Baldrige as secretary of commerce because of his managerial expertise, which contributed to long-term improvement in the efficiency and effectiveness of the corporation he had managed prior to joining the government.

The Malcolm Baldrige National Quality Award is an annual award recognizing U.S. companies that excel in quality management and quality achievement. In February 1993, Secretary of Commerce Ronald Brown announced that the Malcolm Baldrige Quality Award would be expanded to include a category for education. The award criteria are built upon the core values and concepts of:

- Customer-driven quality

- Leadership

- Continuous improvement

- Total participation
- Fast response
- Design quality and prevention
- Long-range outlook
- Management by fact
- Partnership development
- Community responsibility

THE AWARD CRITERIA

As previously mentioned, the award criteria have been customized to be congruent with the unique culture of education. The following is a description of the core values and concepts of the award as customized for education.

Customer-Driven Quality

Customer-driven quality is a strategic concept in education. This core value is based on the belief that the quality of education will improve as students assume more responsibility for the value of education. The attitudes of parents and the community will reflect student perceptions of the value of education. Customer-driven quality is directed toward student achievement. It demands constant sensitivity to emerging student requirements and measurement of the factors that drive student satisfaction. It also demands awareness of the latest developments in education and a rapid response to student requirements. In addition, the school or district's approach to recovering from poor student performance is crucial to improving both the quality of education and the relationships with students, parents, and the community.

Leadership

School board members, administrators, and teachers must create clear and visible quality values within the education system. Reinforcement of values and expectations requires everyone's personal commitment and involvement. School board members and administrators, with participation from teachers, must create strategies, systems, and methods for achieving educational excellence. The systems and methods guide all activities and decisions of the school and district and encourage participation and creativity by all staff and students. Through their regular personal involvement in visible activities, such as planning, review of educational quality performance standards, and recognizing staff for quality achievement, school board members and administrators serve as role models who reinforce the values and encourage leadership at all levels.

Continuous Improvement

The district must have a well-defined and well-executed approach to continuous improvement. Improvement must take place in all parts of the education system. There are several types of improvement:

- Enhance the value of education to students through the development of new educational services

- Reduce inconsistencies that place the credibility of educational processes in question

- Improve responsiveness to student requirements

- Improve productivity and effectiveness in the use of all resources

To meet these objectives, the process of continuous improvement must contain regular cycles of planning, execution, and evaluation.

Total Participation

Meeting the district's quality and performance objectives is everyone's responsibility. Reward and recognition systems must reinforce full participation in the district's quality objectives. Factors bearing upon the safety, health, well-being, and morale of staff and students must be part of the continuous improvement objectives and activities of the district. Students must receive education and training in quality skills related to performing their work and understanding problem-solving tools and techniques.

Fast Response

A fast response to customer requirements is a major quality attribute. Educational processes must be designed to meet both quality and response goals. Improved response time should be included as a major focus within all quality improvement processes. This requires that all designs, objectives, and team activities include measurement of responsiveness. Major improvements in response time may require educational processes and paths to be simplified and shortened. Improvement in response time often drives simultaneous improvements in quality and productivity.

Design Quality and Prevention

Educational quality programs should place a strong emphasis on problem prevention achieved through building quality into every educational process. Excellent design quality will lead to major reductions in downstream waste, problems, and associated costs. Design quality includes the creation of fault-tolerant processes and procedures which take into consideration the customer's changing requirements. Consistent with the theme of design quality and prevention, continuous improvement and corrective action need to emphasize interventions upstream—at the earliest stages in the education cycle.

Long-Range Outlook

Achieving quality requires a future orientation and long-term commitment to staff, students, citizens, and suppliers. Strategies, plans, and resource allocations need to reflect these commitments and address training, staff and student development, supplier development, technology evolution, and other factors that have a bearing on quality. A key part of the long-term commitment is regular review and assessment of progress relative to long-term plans.

Management by Fact

Meeting the quality and performance goals of the school and district requires that process management be based upon reliable information, data, and analysis. The types of data needed for quality assessment and quality improvement include:

- Student performance

- Staff attitudes

- Educational program performance

- Operations

- Benchmarking

- Supplier performance

- Cost and financial analysis

Facts and data analysis support a variety of educational purposes such as planning, reviewing performance, improving procedures, and benchmarking educational quality performance with other schools and commercial enterprises.

A major consideration relating to the use of data and analysis to improve educational performance involves the creation and use of performance indicators. **Performance indicators** are measurable characteristics of educational processes and procedures used by a district to deliver services to students. The indicators are also used to track performance and evaluate progress in achieving continuous improvement. A system of indicators tied to student and district performance requirements represents a clear and objective basis for aligning all activities of the district toward common goals.

Partnership Development

Schools should seek to build internal and external partnerships that serve mutual and larger community interests. Such partnerships might include those that promote labor–management cooperation such as agreements with unions, cooperation with suppliers and students, and linkages with other education organizations and businesses that serve the community. Partnerships should consider longer-term objectives as well as short-term needs, thereby creating a basis for mutual investment. The building of partnerships should address means of regular communication, approaches to evaluating progress, means for modifying objectives, and methods to accommodate changing conditions.

Community Responsibility

Quality objectives for education should reflect areas of community citizenship and responsibility. These include ethics in education, support for public health and safety, support for environmental safety, and sharing of quality-related information with business, schools, and government agencies within the state and community. Health, safety, and environmental considerations need to take into account the life cycle of products and services and include factors such as waste generation. Educational quality plans should include responsiveness to community needs and processes in order to develop and maintain public trust. In addition, the educational quality plan should reflect the district's limited resources, community activities, and the sharing of quality-related information.

The Criteria Framework

The criteria framework (see next page) includes four basic elements: driver, system, measures of progress, and goal. The following is an explanation of the Malcolm Baldrige National Quality Award criteria framework as developed for education:

- **Driver:** School board members, administrators, and teachers create the values, goals, and procedures that guide the sustained pursuit of quality and performance objectives.

- **System:** The system comprises the set of well-defined and well-designed processes for meeting the district's quality and performance requirements.

- **Measures of Progress:** Measures of progress provide a results-oriented basis for documenting, assessing, and channeling actions.

- **Goal:** The basic aim of the quality process is the delivery of ever-increasing value to students and the community.

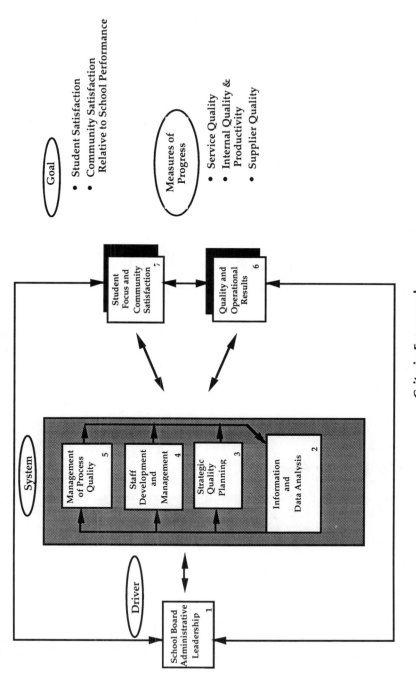

Goal

- Student Satisfaction
- Community Satisfaction Relative to School Performance

Measures of Progress

- Service Quality
- Internal Quality & Productivity
- Supplier Quality

System

Management of Process Quality 5

Staff Development and Management 4

Strategic Quality Planning 3

Information and Data Analysis 2

Student Focus and Community Satisfaction 7

Quality and Operational Results 6

Driver

School Board Administrative Leadership 1

Criteria Framework

WHY SHOULD SCHOOLS IMPLEMENT THE MALCOLM BALDRIGE NATIONAL QUALITY AWARD ASSESSMENT PROCESS?

What Does Assessment Mean?

The Baldrige definition of assessment is non-threatening. The quality definition of assessment is:

- Ensuring that what is supposed to happen actually happens
- Ensuring that everything we do has added value
- Ensuring that what we do provides value to the customer
- Ensuring that we work efficiently
- Ensuring that we constantly strive to improve our output
- Ensuring that we are never resistant to change

Assessment is ensuring that we get the right results. It is everyone's job in the school or district to ensure that what is done is done right the first time and every time. Assessment needs to take place before, during, and after tasks are completed. In some schools, assessment involves everyone. However, this is the exception. Generally, assessment only involves the stakeholders in a process. Everyone in the school or district should use the assessment process as a learning experience.

What Needs to Be Assessed?

Everything done in education should be assessed. We need to determine if what we are doing is:

- Meeting student needs
- Meeting community needs
- Meeting staff needs

Assessment ensures that corrective action is based on data. If the district, school, student, staff, or community is not getting what they expected or needed, changes are made to the process. People are not blamed. Rather, improvements are made to the process to ensure a higher quality output. Assessment should include:

- Simple record keeping
- Target setting at all levels and for all activities
- Ongoing processes
- Feedback processes
- Activity analysis

What Are the Benefits?

The benefits of applying the Malcolm Baldrige National Quality Award criteria to your school and/or district are:

- The establishment of a culture in education that focuses on meeting the needs of students
- A staff that is involved, informed, and motivated to constantly improve the quality of every educational process
- Increased cooperation at all levels
- The creation of better learning and working environments for all
- Improved efficiency and productivity by all
- Improved student and administrative outcomes
- Effective teamwork by all stakeholders
- Improvements in education recognized by community, staff, and students

Meeting the Malcolm Baldrige National Quality Award criteria will enable schools to meet their strategic aims. This is essential if the quality of education is going to improve. Schools must turn out productive citizens who possess the skills and motivation necessary to meet today's business demands. Education is all about people, and the process of achieving educational success through people is the foundation of the Malcolm Baldrige National Quality Award criteria as applied to education.

Today, education is under intense pressure to change. Restructuring programs are being implemented to improve teacher performance, to enhance the curriculum, to demand more of students, and to improve school tone. These efforts to change education have met with limited success because they have a very narrow view of education. Quality, on the other hand, views education as a total system, made up of numerous internal and external components. Only by improving the entire educational system can education professionals make the improvements demanded by society. The Malcolm Baldrige National Quality Award is a tool that education professionals can use to unite the components of education into a cohesive system that focuses on continuous improvement.

CHAPTER 4

TQM IN EDUCATION

In this chapter, the concepts previously discussed are further expanded. We will learn a new definition of quality that is based on the "pillars of quality" in the Total Quality School model. The pillars are the foundation for the transformation to quality. Each pillar supports the cultural transformation that schools must undergo to achieve a quality culture. Achieving a quality culture in education and, for that matter, in any organization is hard work that is accomplished over a long period of time. Dr. W. Edwards Deming insists that it takes five years before an organization realizes any benefits from the quality effort.

Unfortunately, education professionals cannot wait five years to demonstrate the benefits of quality. Therefore, a major component of this approach to implementing quality is the development of a measurement system that enables every education professional to document and measure the added value of their quality initiative. This enables educators to measure the effectiveness of their quality programs and to demonstrate the added value of education to the community. Many schools are working to rapidly change their environments to improve every educational processes in order to improve outcomes and reduce costs.

A Total Quality School is based upon the fact that everyone involved in the education process holds similar beliefs and values. Most

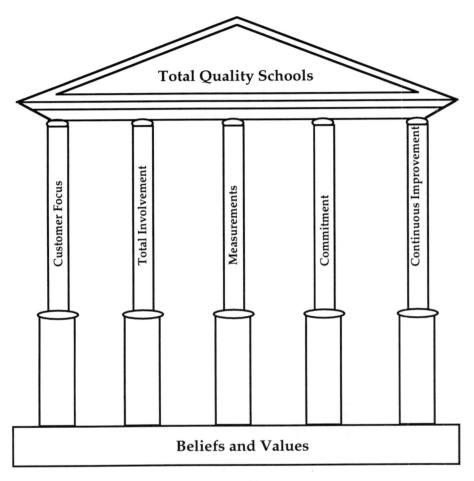

Total Quality Schools Model

education professionals enter the field of education because they want to contribute to the growth and development of children. Unfortunately, their beliefs and values have become overshadowed by the current economic climate and the drive by many communities to have their school systems copy business practices to increase efficiency and reduce costs.

Becoming a Total Quality School requires building a close relationship with your customers. Education provides a service that has the potential to solve many of today's important problems in society. The public education professional must develop new, improved ways of teaching. If the current education system is to survive its current crisis, today's public school systems must finish first in the race to provide society with graduates who can meet today's academic and business challenges.

Students have many different problems. Unfortunately, schools have limited resources. Instead of trying to solve all of the students' problems, educators must focus on solving the right problem. Identifying the right problem is one of the major challenges for today's teachers and administrators. In education, the right problem is the problem that is preventing the student from succeeding in the classroom.

How would you define excellent performance for your school or district? How does your school or district contribute to the success of the student and society? These are the questions that a Total Quality School must be able to answer. Society does not want to continue to buy the same educational systems that have existed for the past century. Society is demanding that education professionals become leaders in developing programs that enable every student to succeed.

CHARACTERISTICS OF A TOTAL QUALITY SCHOOL

Initially, a quality school has five characteristics, identified as the pillars of quality, as depicted in the illustration on the next page. (As your school develops a quality philosophy, you will be able to identify five additional characteristics of a quality school.) These pillars are based on the school's beliefs such as trust, cooperation, and leadership.

Quality in education requires a commitment to customer satisfaction and a commitment to creating an environment in which staff and students can do their best work. However, before you can develop a Total Quality School, you must understand what each pillar represents.

Customer Focus

In a Total Quality School, everyone is both a customer and a supplier. The school's customers are primarily students and their families, or *Big-C* customers. They are the main beneficiaries of school work. Parents are initially classified as *Big-C* customers because of their concern for their

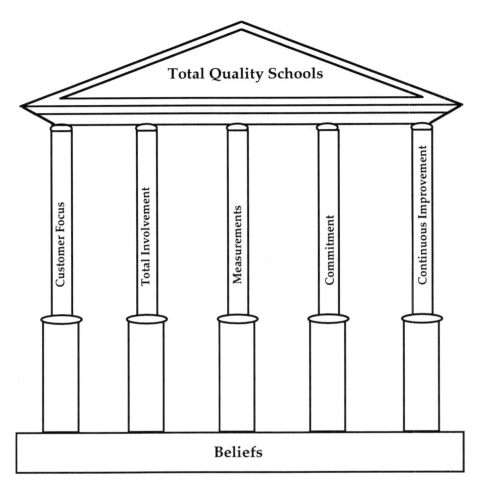

Characteristics of a Total Quality School

child's education. However, as the student matures, the parents make the transition to *little-c* customers. This allows the student to take more responsibility for his or her education.

Parents are also suppliers to the education system. Parents provide the Total Quality School with students who are ready to learn. It is the responsibility of the Total Quality School to work with parents to optimize the student's potential to benefit from the learning processes provided at the school. An excellent example of this relationship is Souhegan High School in Amherst, New Hampshire. Souhegan High School has implemented a program to help parents better understand how they can improve the education their child receives by participating in the education process. Staff regularly meet with parents at home to discuss their student's academic accomplishments and areas for improvement. Together, they develop a learning plan for the student that is designed to maximize the student's strengths and minimize the potential for failure.

Schools have both internal and external customers. **Internal customers** are the parents, students, teachers, administrators, staff, and school board. They are within the education system. **External customers** are society, employers, families, the military, and higher education. They are external to the organization. However, they use the output of the education process.

It is appropriate here to introduce the concept of a **customer/supplier chain**. A relationship exists between what your customer expects of you and what you expect of your supplier. It is your customer's responsibility to clearly identify his or her requirements. It is your responsibility to translate your customer's requirements into supplier specifications. You cannot meet your customer's requirements unless your supplier provides you with material that meets your requirements. Unfortunately, this concept is lost in education; however, it applies to every educational process. For example, a sixth grade teacher expects incoming students to possess certain levels of knowledge. If a student lacks the required knowledge, the sixth grade teacher must readjust his or her teaching program to accommodate the student's requirements. Oftentimes, this means that the teacher must repeat material that should have been covered in the fifth grade. This is an example of a breakdown in the customer/supplier chain.

Total Involvement

Everyone must participate in the quality transformation. Quality is not just the school board or superintendent's responsibility. It is everyone's responsibility. Quality demands that everyone contribute to the quality effort.

Measurement

This is an area where most schools fail. Many good things are happening in education today, but the education professionals involved in the process become so focused on solving problems that they fail to measure the effectiveness of their efforts. In other words, you can't improve what you can't measure. Schools cannot meet the quality standards established by society unless they have a vehicle for measuring progress toward achieving those standards. Students use test scores to measure their progress in a class. Communities use school budgets to measure the efficiency of school processes.

Commitment

The superintendent of schools and the school board must be committed to quality. If they are not, the quality transformation process should not be initiated, because it will fail. Everyone needs to support the quality effort. Quality is a cultural change that causes an organization to change the way things are done. People are resistant to change, and management must support the change process by providing people with the education, tools, systems, and processes that promote quality.

Continuous Improvement

This topic will be discussed in greater detail in Chapter 14. However, the point is that schools must do things better tomorrow than they did yesterday or do today. Education professionals must constantly be on the lookout for ways to prevent problems from occurring; they must correct process problems as they develop and make improvements.

APPLYING YOUR KNOWLEDGE: EXERCISE

We have discussed the meaning of the pillars in a Total Quality School. Now take a closer look at what the pillars mean to your school or district.

Step 1:	In a team setting, discuss the strengths and weaknesses of your school. Review the list below.
Step 2:	Develop a list of the strengths and weaknesses of your school or district. (Use the form on the next page.)
Step 3:	Present your list to others. You might want to record the lists prepared by others.

Total Quality Schools

Pillars of Quality	Strengths	Weaknesses
Customer Focus	We regularly meet with staff, students, parents, and representatives of the community to define their requirements.	We don't respond to staff, student, parent or community concerns/complaints.
Total Involvement	Staff has the shared responsibility to solve problems as they develop.	Generally, the staff waits for management and others to solve problems.
Measurement	We collect data to measure our improvements and to develop solutions.	We don't track our progress. We just go on to the next issue.
Commitment	Management is committed to providing people with the training, systems, and processes they need to change the way they work to improve quality and increase productivity.	Support for quality is isolated and not recognized by the staff, students or community.
Continuous Improvement	We are constantly looking for ways to improve every educational process.	We are content with things as they are and unless there is a problem we don't address an issue.

Total Quality Schools

Pillars of Quality	Strengths	Weaknesses
Customer Focus		
Total Involvement		
Measurement		
Commitment		
Continuous Improvement		

HOW QUALITY SUPPORTS
THE SCHOOL IMPROVEMENT PROCESS

The graph presented below was developed to demonstrate to the staff of the Richmond County Public Schools how quality can be used to achieve the objectives of the district's school improvement program. This graph helped the staff to understand that quality is not just another program, but that it provides the tools and techniques that they will need to implement their school improvement program.

Both the quality and school improvement models develop a systems view of education. They focus upon the total school program

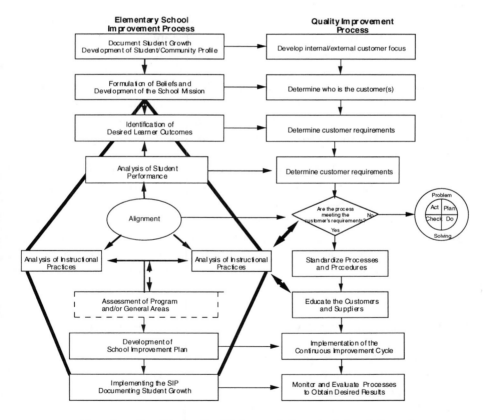

**Mapping Quality to the Richmond County School Board
School Improvement Process**

rather than each of the separate components within that program. Both models recognize the critical importance of collaboratively developed beliefs, mission, and desired learner outcomes. Both models encourage the development of staff/parent consensus for change and the way by which change will be achieved. The models focus on results. They encourage staff and students to identify a variety of measures to describe performance.

The school improvement model and the quality process both seek to identify best practices. Best practices are used as a standard by which all improvement is measured. Both models seek to align organizational practices with achievement of the desired outcomes and the mission of the school. Continuous improvement is a key component of both models. As staff become familiar with the quality and school improvement processes, they identify ways to improve every educational process, from waxing the floor to managing the classroom.

The quality process enhances the school improvement model by providing education professionals with the tools and techniques needed to achieve the desired objectives. Quality focuses on using data to effect change. Evaluation and assessment are key components in both models. Quality provides people with the tools to manage change. Both models strive to become the culture of the organization, the normal way of doing business.

This blend of models is a unique approach that will enable the Richmond County Public Schools to achieve their desired objectives. Quality is not another process. It is a management system that can be used to implement the school improvement model. Quality is a structured process that helps people to develop systems for collecting and analyzing data. Quality helps people to determine if the desired objectives were achieved in order to improve every educational process.

IMPLEMENTING QUALITY IN THE CLASSROOM

The implementation of quality techniques discussed in this book provides you with the tools you need to change your classroom from a teacher-centered focus to a learning/student-centered focus. How is this accomplished? Take a long, hard look at your classroom.

- Are the desks lined up in straight rows?

- Is your desk at the front of the room?
- Do you sit at your desk most of the time?
- Do you lecture from a podium at the front of the room?
- Are materials accessible only to you?
- Is there an emphasis on individual worksheets?
- Is covering the curriculum the most important goal?
- Do your students complain of being bored?
- Do you develop and impose disciplinary procedures?
- Do you discourage interactions between yourself and your students?
- Do you discourage interactions between students in the classroom?
- Do you close the door to "outsiders"?

If you answered yes to all or most of these questions, you have a teacher-centered classroom. In this chapter, you will learn how to change your classroom from a teacher-centered classroom to a student-centered classroom. You will gain the practical knowledge you need to implement quality in your classroom. Teachers have developed model classrooms for elementary, middle, and high schools, and the results have been astounding. Disciplinary problems have been reduced, student performance has improved, and safe learning and working environments have been created.

CLASSROOM DESIGN

One of the easiest and most effective ways to change the focus of your classroom is to change the arrangement of the furniture. If possible, get rid of the desks and bring in tables. Arrange the desks (tables) in a large circle or in groups of four facing each other. Remember, the furniture isn't bolted to the floor in one position. Use it to facilitate what you are doing. Move the furniture around. The students will get used to it—even those who resist any change. Explaining why the furniture is arranged in a particular way makes it easier for the students to accept the change. The arrangement of the furniture sets the tone of the classroom and serves as a visual reminder of the new focus on the students and on learning.

At a staff meeting, one teacher who was implementing quality in her classroom told the other teachers that her classroom was becoming more student-centered. The concept of a student-centered classroom was not easily understood by many of the other teachers. Basically, the teachers argued that all of the classrooms in the school are student-centered learning environments. However, the quality teacher explained that in a student-centered classroom, the students participate in the management of all classroom functions. In a teacher-centered classroom, the teacher is responsible for the management of the classroom. When she asked the other teachers if their classrooms were student-centered, less than 10% responded in the affirmative.

The total impact of the change on this teacher might have been lost had she not begun to co-teach with other members of the school's English department. The quality teacher was assigned to co-teach with another English teacher in the general education department. As the quality teacher entered the classroom of the traditional teacher, she immediately noticed that all of the desks were aligned in rows and that the students were seated alphabetically. The two teachers discussed their differing educational philosophies and decided that their primary goal was to create a cohesive classroom which recognized and celebrated the differences among the students. With some reluctance, the traditional teacher agreed to create a student-centered classroom. The results from this experiment exceeded the expectations of the traditional teacher. The diagram on the next page illustrates the difference between a traditional classroom and a quality classroom.

The class was composed of students from the lowest regular education levels and of educationally handicapped students who generally had been in self-contained (segregated) classrooms all their school careers. The teachers found that the physical setup of the classroom worked against their goal of providing opportunities for the students to get to know and appreciate one another.

Cooperative projects and activities are less likely to be considered with this type of physical arrangement. Student-generated discussions are at best awkward. The most vocal students tend to talk, while the teacher remains at the "center of the action."

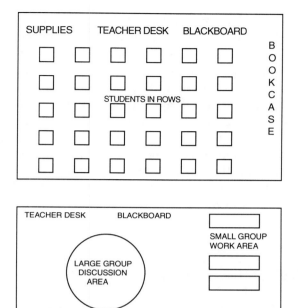

A Traditional vs. a TQM Classroom

Conversely, in the quality classroom, the expectation that all students will work together cooperatively and support one another is supported and encouraged by the physical layout. Teachers who have visited a quality classroom remark positively on the layout, which allows for whole group, small group, and individual work areas.

CURRICULUM ISSUES

The atmosphere or climate in the classroom is equally important. How often have you said something like, "We have to cover this chapter by Friday." These words reveal a teacher-centered classroom where the students are secondary to the curriculum. The learning-centered classroom gives primary consideration to the needs of each student.

A young lady, her parents, her teacher, and a learning specialist who acted as facilitator and recorder attended a meeting at a large high school. The meeting had been called at the request of the parents. The young lady had walked out of the class a few days earlier. The meeting was called to find out why this had happened and what could be done to prevent it from happening again. The young lady was very intelligent, but had some mild learning disabilities and as a result had a low frustration/stress level. She was appropriately placed in a top-level class. As the discussion proceeded, the teacher related that she was unable to stop to answer any questions because she had to "follow the curriculum and be on the same page at the same time as the other teachers teaching this course." Imagine the reaction of the parents. Their daughter had asked a legitimate question to clarify a concept, which the teacher felt she was unable to stop to answer.

APPLYING YOUR KNOWLEDGE: EXERCISE

What kind of classroom is this? What should have been done?

This is a system problem. The student is not the focus of this classroom. The curriculum must be covered or the teacher will incur the wrath of her supervisor. The solution is not to place the student in a lower level class or to have her come for help after school. The solution is to change the focus of the classroom.

How can we expect students to take responsibility for their learning when they have no say in the classroom? Quality does not advocate abdicating your responsibility for what happens in your classroom. Quality does advocate a shared responsibility in the classroom. Quality allows the students to take responsibility for their own learning. Quality connects the classroom to the real world. The teacher directs what is taught, but the students actively participate in the learning process. The students are free to discuss issues and to disagree with the teacher. The students are free to suggest projects and related issues. The students are valued in the classroom.

EVALUATION PROCESS

The students are part of the evaluative process as well. Evaluation must extend beyond the traditional tests which only evaluate how many facts can be spewed back. Evaluation must begin to consider process as well as product.

Students must begin to take responsibility for assessing how much they have really learned, how they can apply this knowledge, and where improvements can be made. Most of us have crammed for a test and then promptly forgotten the information. We have all been unprepared for something at some time because we had not recognized the need to pay attention. Only the individual really knows how much he or she has learned.

A model quality English class recently read a story about a student who failed a civics class despite having done all the work and having an A average. It seems that the student walked downtown with the teacher one day after school. The student blithely threw peanut shells along the way and disposed of the bag on the courthouse lawn. A week later, she received her report card with an F in civics. Certain that a mistake had been made, she went to see the teacher. Despite her arguments, he maintained that she had not learned the unit on "keeping your town clean." The teacher said, "Never say you've learned something until it makes a change in your life."

In a quality classroom, students debated not the issue of what was learned, but the fairness of this grade. Some maintained that the student had "failed" the last test (the walk downtown). Others said that it was unfair to be marked on something that happened outside of school. Others maintained that the student had cheated on the previous tests. Only a few agreed with the teacher that the student had not learned the material.

Grades have a disproportionate place in the education system. Learning is secondary or even irrelevant to the acquisition of the grade. How often do you hear students comparing their grades—and putting each other down in the process?

One way to involve students in focusing on what is learned is to have them help determine the criteria by which they will be graded. Students can also be involved in evaluating their own work as well as that of others.

Many projects lend themselves to student-established criteria. Generally, quality classes work on cooperative projects. For example, students in one class were assigned a project to design or modify a board game for use by sighted and blind children. Once the students were given the project outcomes, they were able to decide on the following criteria:

- The game should be fun to play.
- The game should have clear, easy-to-follow rules.
- The game should specify how many players are needed.
- The game should have appropriate equipment.
- The blind players should require as little help as possible to play the game.

The students presented their games to the class, other students, staff, parents, etc. The students knew exactly how their product would be judged.

In a quality classroom, a project that is attempted should not receive a failing grade. (The only way to fail is not to do the project at all.) Some quality teachers use a four-part rating scale (excellent = A, good = B, fair = C, poor = D) which allows for ease in converting to grade scores and provides a passing grade floor. Each student is given a form, and all assessments are equal. Each criterion is judged separately; a grade is determined for the project. This grade is shared by the whole group. A separate individual grade is earned through the demonstration of targeted behaviors. This method of grading seems to alleviate some of the parental and student concerns about fairness. The student who works hard on the project earns two good grades, while the student who contributes little earns one good grade (for the project) and a lesser grade corresponding to the contribution he or she made.

A checklist or daily group observation form helps the students to become more aware of what they are doing. A daily observation can be modified for any age group. For young students, simple questions and smiling or frowning faces are appropriate. For older students, a multiple-choice format is useful. Open-ended questions provoke reflection by older students but present greater difficulty in converting to grade scores.

FOR YOUNG STUDENTS: The teacher asks questions such as, "How do you feel about what your group did today?" "Did you share the work?" "Were you nice to the others in your group?" Answers can be indicated through the use of smiley faces.

FOR MIDDLE STUDENTS: Circle the phrase that best describes what happened today in your group.

How much did the group get done?
        a lot   quite a bit   some   not much   none

Did your group make good choices?
                yes   mostly   fair   hardly   no

Who contributed ideas?
        everyone   almost all   some   not too many   no one

FOR OLDER STUDENTS: Open-ended questions or a numerical rating system works well.

Open-ended questions can include "What did the group do today?" "How were tasks delegated?" "What problems cropped up and how were they handled?"

A numerical rating system may be used effectively and lends itself to easy conversion to grades:

Circle the number which describes your efforts
(0 = excellent through 6 = poor)

Sorts information effectively	10	9	8	7	6
Asks good, probing questions	10	9	8	7	6
Adds to ideas being discussed	10	9	8	7	6

This checklist or observation form provides the documentation for further individual improvement. It is not enough to say that a student's problem-solving skills are weak. It is much more helpful to identify and set goals for specific areas, such as being able to restate the problem or being able to brainstorm different possibilities. Using this format provides each student with immediate feedback and puts the responsibility for change squarely on the shoulders of the individual student. This, of course, does not imply that the teacher does not provide support and encouragement for each student.

Students should also be asked to give themselves a grade for the marking period. This grade includes test scores, daily work, effort, and behavior. Students are further asked to justify their choices. They are also asked to share what they have learned in the class. To preempt a response of "nothing," students are told that if they did not learn anything, they should receive a failing grade and should give serious consideration to the reasons why they are in school. Surprisingly, these "grades" from special education students in a self-contained classroom can be very close to the teacher's calculations and reveal a fair amount of honest introspection.

DISCIPLINE ISSUES

"I am the teacher. I make the decisions. **You** do what I say because I say so." Have you ever heard yourself say these words? Have you ever asked yourself, "How can I teach when I have to spend all my time on discipline?"

The problems in the classroom used to be chewing gum and running in the halls. Now the problems are violence, drug and alcohol abuse, racial animosity, and sexual harassment. Chewing gum in class is not a problem in the real world of education in the 1990s.

Educators know that some of the problems today's students bring with them into the classroom cannot be solved in the classroom. The problems are too large and complex. The causes are beyond the control of any classroom teacher. We cannot provide solutions but we can provide support and empathy. Teachers can show respect for students who often do not respect themselves or anyone else. Teachers can uphold high expectations for behavior and knowledge.

The following poem was written by an autistic student. It speaks eloquently to the need of all students for acceptance and respect.

A People Place

William J. Crockett (with thanks to Ken Medena)—for Cleve

If this is not a place where tears are understood,
Where do I go to cry?

If this is not a place where my spirits can take wing,
  Where do I go to fly?

If this is not a place where my questions can be asked,
  Where do I go to seek?

If this is not a place where my feelings can be heard,
  Where do I go to speak?

If this is not a place where you will accept me as I am,
  Where do I go to be?

If this is not a place where I can try to learn and grow,
  Where can I just be me?

If this is not a place where tears are understood,
  Where can I go to cry?

Students often need someone to believe in them and to listen to them. The teacher is often that someone. Every classroom should be a safe haven, where each student is valued for his or her unique abilities and where each student is encouraged to take the risk of learning.

Educators can relinquish the omnipotent, omniscient role that is so easy to assume. We can acknowledge our humanity, our fallibility. Students are more likely to respect a teacher who admits that he or she might be wrong but still does what he or she perceives as right. None of us likes to be told what to do. If we have a say in what happens, we are more likely to accept what has to be. We prefer to have choices. Students also should have a choice or a say in what they do.

Quality gives students an opportunity to share responsibility for their learning. The teacher does not abdicate his or her role, but instead shares joint responsibility for the conduct of the classroom. With choice and responsibility come consequences. Failure may be a consequence and should be acknowledged.

One teacher had the proverbial "class from hell." Nothing seemed to work. The students were rude, disrespectful, did not want to do any assignment, and did not want to work alone or with others. The students seemed to delight in harassing each other and the teacher in particular. The teacher tried everything she could think of. Nothing seemed to effect any lasting change. Unfortunately, the teacher fell into the trap of negativity and couldn't wait for that class to be over.

Finally, the teacher understood that none of the students were invested in the class. The teacher said, "If only I could convince them to take ownership of the problem." The teacher adopted a quality philosophy. She told the students that she refused to continue as "policeman," trying to catch them doing wrong and then punishing them. She asked them to identify the problem and to suggest solutions. The problem centered around discipline. The proposed solutions focused solely on punishments. It took much effort to get the students to present positive statements to follow. The statements were then posted. Each student wrote a personal goal in his or her journal. The teacher's goal was to "catch them being good" and to reward that behavior.

We would like to say that this experiment was a resounding success, but that would be quite an exaggeration. The best that can be reported is that the incidence of good behavior increased and the class became more bearable for everyone. When you are at the bottom, the improvements are small and at first transient. If they are recognized, they can provide a foundation for further improvements over time.

Some classes are very difficult and challenging. Documentation helps to identify the problem and to highlight the improvements. What we perceive as the problem may only be a symptom. If we attack the symptom instead of the underlying cause, we are like the rug merchant in the Sufi parable:

> Once there was a rug merchant who saw that his most beautiful carpet had a large bump in its center. He stepped on the bump to flatten it out—and succeeded. But the bump reappeared in a new spot not far away. He jumped on the bump again, and it disappeared—for a moment, until it emerged once more in a new place. Again and again he jumped, scuffing and mangling the rug in his frustration; until finally he lifted one corner of the carpet and an angry snake slithered out.
>
> *(from The Fifth Discipline).*

There are causes which are within our control and those which are not. We must have the wisdom to know the difference so we can concentrate on those things which we are able to change.

Think again about how a student-centered classroom would look and feel. Which of the following statements apply to your classroom?

- The furniture is arranged to facilitate group interactions.
- Students rearrange furniture to suit projects.
- All equipment is readily accessible.
- Everyone respects the property of others.
- I am supportive and empathetic toward troubled students.
- The students are interested in what they are doing.
- The students take responsibility for their actions.
- The classroom is a safe place for all students.

INCLUSION

PL 94-142 and the Americans with Disabilities Act are drastically changing the face of education in America. The closed doors of special education classrooms and of institutions have opened. Children we never dreamed would be sitting in our classrooms are there before us expecting to receive a free and appropriate education with their peers.

Do these students fit into a quality equation? The answer is an unequivocal yes. A quality education is an inclusive education. Quality assumes that all students are capable of and willing to do quality work. Schools are for **all** students, not just some. Our diversity is our strength. The greater our diversity, the more powerful our ability to create new visions. We are challenged to rethink the routine and purpose of our classrooms. The solution is to provide learning opportunities for all students, to raise students up instead of "water down" the curriculum or lower our expectations.

The foundation of quality is respect—respect for ourselves as professionals and respect for all the children in our classrooms. You cannot fake respect; it comes from within.

Honestly examine your beliefs:

- Are all people equal in value?
- Is it feasible to provide equal opportunity?
- Should we choose and train an "elite" to take care of the rest?
- Can all people/children learn?

- Do all people have unique contributions to make?
- Do children benefit from being with those who are "different"?

These are not easy questions. They strike at the heart of our individual value systems. As educators we know full well the difficulty of teaching to a diverse population. We know the fear of having a disabled or perhaps a non-verbal child in our classroom. Teachers know the uncertainty of deciding what to teach, how to provide equality of opportunity, and how to recognize and deal with vastly differing capabilities.

Quality provides a framework for continuous improvement in the classroom, for respect coupled with high expectations for all students, and techniques to achieve these goals. Each student is acknowledged as an important individual who has social, emotional, and intellectual needs. Education is personalized according to learning styles, and students are afforded the opportunity to benefit from a leadership role as well as meet the challenge of working in a cooperative role. The **best** is expected from **each and every** student.

THE TEACHER

Teachers are the mediators
who provide or fail to provide the essential experiences
that permit students to release their awesome potential.

Asa Hilliard III

Personal Change

Previously, we discussed taking control of our professional and personal lives and deciding to restructure our classrooms to focus on quality principles, practices, and procedures. We began to define quality and the benefits that accrue from implementation. We also discussed the importance of the physical layout of our classrooms and the change from a teacher-centered to a learning-centered classroom. We will now focus on our attitudes and the methods we employ.

With all the demands made upon teachers, it is easy to lose sight of what is really important. It is easy to get bogged down by the paperwork, to say yes instead of no, to lose focus. When teachers lose sight of what is important and spend too much time and effort on tasks that are unimportant and/or impossible to do, they set themselves up for burnout.

A teacher's time and energy can be expended wisely; teachers can make choices based on their values. The curriculum is often determined by the district or the department. Great public debate rages over the allocation of resources in education. Taxes go up, and more money is funneled into the education system, yet test scores continue to decline and students who are functionally illiterate still graduate. The court system and legislators tell us that it is the fault of teachers when students do not learn. They say that no student is "unmotivated." It is the teacher's fault for not using methods which access that student's learning style.

To fail is the ultimate disgrace in education. Teachers are expected never to fail—and certainly never to admit it if the "unthinkable" does happen. To admit failure or even ask for help is to be seen as less competent than other teachers. Yet trying innovative strategies in the classroom requires taking risks and being open to the possibility, even the probability, of failure. No child learns to walk without first crawling. The first steps are tentative; the security of a hand to hold helps to build confidence. But always there are falls, tears, and hurts.

Implementing a new attitude and approach to teaching is much like learning to walk. Failure will happen. It is important to build a support system. Talk to other teachers. Learn what went wrong and find out how to make it right. Slow and steady improvement is the key. There is no magic wand or magic words that produce instantaneous results. We become proficient and competent by implementing quality continuously.

Teachers have limited control over time, curriculum, resources and learning styles but can control the physical layout of the classroom, the attitudes that are both modelel and encouraged, and the methods that are used.

Personal Attitude

A third grade teacher asks, "Why didn't they tell me when I began my teacher training that children learn by talking and working together?" A graduate student intern laments, "They didn't teach me *anything* about managing a whole classroom full of students."

These teachers have begun to question their roles in the classroom. They have begun the paradigm shift required for quality. The teacher in the quality classroom is a facilitator and coach as opposed to a dispenser of knowledge. The students, through the strategy of teaming, take responsibility for their own learning. The curriculum shares equal priority with the acquisition of thinking/living skills. Students learn how to think instead of being taught what to think. The teacher must be able to observe and to give concrete feedback to the students. The teacher must truly believe in what he or she is doing and in the inherent value of each and every person.

Verbalizing the intent to become more of a coach or facilitator is the first step, and one of the easier ones. Breaking old habits is the more difficult part. Videotaping can be a useful tool to analyze our role in the classroom. Observation by a peer is also helpful. One teacher, after watching a videotape of his classroom, remarked that he had no idea how much he dominated and directed student activity.

It is difficult to become accustomed to questioning and encouraging student exploration of ideas. It is much easier to give an answer than it is to ask a question that will elicit thought on the part of the students. It is much easier to ask a factual recall question than it is to ask a question that requires thought. Bloom's Taxonomy provides a framework for asking probing questions and can be used in all grades with all ability levels:

- **Knowledge:** Recalling basic facts about a topic

- **Comprehension:** Understanding the facts about the topic

- **Application:** Using facts to solve problems or making use of facts in a new way

- **Analysis:** Examining facts in relationship to each other or in relationship to larger/different issues/situations

- **Synthesis:** Creating new or original ideas or products based on an understanding of the facts

- **Evaluation:** Judging the value of information, ideas, or products

Using Bloom's Taxonomy stretches the minds of students. The results can be surprising. As undergraduate education students, we all learned how expectations can determine outcomes. Keeping our expectations high yet realistic takes some practice. But it is better to have expectations that are too high than too low.

Some teachers spend their teaching careers in front of the classroom lecturing. Many students memorize enough answers to pass the course; others do not and fail. "It's good enough," these teachers might say. Even the students and their parents might agree. But "good enough" is not good enough anymore. Being shortsighted has cost us dearly.

Much of the current literature focuses on raising the self-esteem of students. There are even specific curricula to follow. Quality treats self-esteem as an integral part of the quality approach. Self-esteem is not raised by insincere irrelevant "touchy-feely" praise for poor or mediocre work. Students instinctively know when they are being patronized. They internalize the message that they are incompetent and "losers." Once internalized, this message leaves an indelible mark.

Self-esteem is raised, instead, by building competency, by recognizing slow and steady improvement, by allowing students to take ownership of their learning. True self-esteem comes only from within.

Changing policy and/or structure does not create change in the classroom. Teachers will not commit to a new program just because it is the "latest word" in teaching. Real change is based in the values and principles of the people in the organization. People, students, and staff will commit their energy to ideals which transcend the individual.

Teachers begin to see themselves as an integral part of the school structure. They begin to discover ways to collaborate and to make improvements. They seek ways to meet individual student needs instead of trying to fit all students into the existing rigid structure. Flexibility, openness, and creativity are hallmarks of the quality teacher. The quality teacher is able to respond to new challenges, adapt to changing demands, and be true to his or her values and principles.

The principal goal of education is to create men who are capable of doing new things, not simply of repeating what other generations have done—men who are creative, inventive and discoverers. The second goal of education is to form minds which can be critical, can verify, and not accept everything they are offered.

Jean Piaget

APPLYING YOUR KNOWLEDGE: EXERCISE

If you think that what you have been doing is good enough, reflect on the words of Jean Piaget and think again.

What could you improve?

What could you do better?

What is within your control to change?

PARENTAL INVOLVEMENT

Study after study identifies parental involvement as crucial to a student's success in school. Unfortunately, few studies describe effective means to increase parental involvement. Economic conditions often determine the level of parental support. Quality welcomes the involvement of parents in the classroom on problem-solving teams and as equal partners in the educational process. In the quality paradigm, parents are both suppliers (of students) and customers (as members of society who ultimately benefit from students' educational attainment and subsequent employment).

Parents are often victims of economic circumstances which prevent a more active role in education. All parents want to see their children succeed in school. Some parents have to contend with their own negative memories of school. Over the years, they may become more discouraged and less willing to support school personnel. While teachers cannot wave a magic wand and change circumstances, we can encourage parents to support education. Teachers can open the doors to the building and the classroom. Teachers can encourage communication and understanding of mutually supportive roles in the lives of students.

Parents and the community cannot be left in the dark in terms of what happens in the classroom. A letter sent home at the beginning of the year is helpful to establish communication. Quality is a vastly different approach to education. Everyone has gone to school, and thus everyone is an "expert." Not only do students and staff need training and knowledge about quality, but communication with parents is essential for success. Some parents may, by virtue of their employment, be involved with quality. These parents can be valuable resources. It is, however, important to recognize the differences between the cultures of education and business.

Teachers have extensive contact with parents—most positive, some negative. It is easy to fall into an adversarial position when a parent storms into a classroom and angrily complains that his or her child got a failing grade or was unfairly treated or…the list goes on and on. It is easy to become angry when parents or community members complain about teacher salaries and cite the problems in education. The quality approach does not point fingers or place blame. Quality identifies the problems and seeks workable solutions.

Quality can have far-reaching effects on students and their parents. The problem-solving approach equally emphasizes providing optimum learning opportunities and student responsibility. One parent angrily called a teacher to complain that her daughter was not doing well in class. The teacher, parent, and student met to define the problem. The student began and listed a number of things which the teacher perceived as presenting difficulty. They all reached consensus on defining the problem. They brainstormed as a group to come up with a number of different solutions. They prioritized the solutions and determined the most appropriate one for the student as well as the teacher. The student and the teacher both saw the other's point of view and each made some concessions. The outcome of this session was that the student's attitude and performance improved. The parent started allowing the student more freedom to make decisions and adopted a less active role as advocate for her daughter.

CHAPTER 5

QUALITY

What is quality? Quality is a structured process for improving the output produced. It is neither magical nor complex. Quality is based on common sense. Dr. W. Edwards Deming's quality management philosophy was developed out of a necessity to improve the working conditions for every employee. When Dr. Deming began his career in the 1920s, he encountered a management environment that thrived on fear. This environment exists in many of our schools today.

Quality focuses on the positive efforts put forth by an individual. In the 1920s, an employee could work all day and not receive any pay because the assembly line did not produce marketable product. Using the quality methodology, every work system can be divided into a series of work processes, as depicted in the following model:

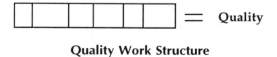 = Quality

Quality Work Structure

Each work series is a unique process that contributes to the creation of the output. In a quality school, a quality standard is established for each work series within the overall work process. If the worker achieves the quality standard for each work series, the end result is a quality product. Quality eliminates the need for after-the-fact inspection. Where is after-the-fact inspection used in education today?

When people talk about improving the quality of education, often what they are talking about is improving student grades or scores. In these types of schools, the responsibility for improving the quality of education rests with the teacher. Teachers generally focus on only one aspect of a student's education: helping the student learn and retain knowledge. When quality begins as an isolated project in a school or classroom, it is less likely to influence the overall quality of education.

For example, one teacher has been actively implementing quality in her classroom for the past seven years. She was instrumental in helping another teacher develop his understanding of quality. However, the quality effort at the school has been confined to the quality teacher's classroom. Many of her fellow teachers are reluctant to accept the quality challenge. This type of implementation of quality is called *little-q* quality.

In contrast, *Big-Q* quality schools make everyone responsible for quality. People are provided with the tools they need to change the way they work in order to improve the quality of their output. People are responsible for reducing waste and inefficiency. As a result of their effort, they create a better learning and working environment.

An excellent example of a *Big-Q* quality school is Region 3 Technical High School in Lincoln, Maine. Everyone at Region 3 is responsible for quality. The school board has adopted a quality focus that encourages staff, students, and parents to develop innovative teaching and learning programs that better prepare students to meet future academic and business challenges. Quality has moved from the classroom to administrative functions. The school board has adopted quality procedures to govern board meetings.

THE PRINCIPLES OF QUALITY

Quality is the most important topic of discussion in education today. There are probably as many different ideas about quality as there are schools. Quality is creating an environment where educators, parents, government officials, community representatives, and business leaders work together to provide students with the resources they need to meet current and future academic, business, and societal challenges. To begin the discussion, let's look at what quality means to you.

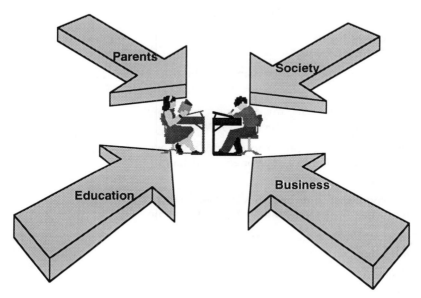

Quality Focus for Education

The following survey is a simple tool that can be used to determine your district or school's Phase of Quality. The focus of quality is on consistently meeting or exceeding internal and external customer requirements. The Phases of Quality module can be used to help identify the cultural facilitators or barriers that affect the implementation of quality in your school or district.

SURVEY OF SELECTED PRINCIPLES FOR A QUALITY ORGANIZATION

Column #1 Personally agree with the principles
Scoring: 0 (strongly disagree) to 5 (strongly agree)

Column #2 Organization practices the principle
Scoring: 0 (don't ever do it) to 5 (always do it)

Column #3 Department practices the principle
Scoring: 0 (don't ever do it) to 5 (always do it)

Principles	#1	#2	#3
1. Quality work and results are the priority for me and for the people I work with.	____	___	____
2. Delighting the external customer is a high priority for me and for the people I work with.	____	___	____
3. Delighting the internal customer is a high priority for me and for the people I work with.	____	___	____
4. I collect data to make my decisions, and this is true for the majority of people I work with.	____	___	____
5. I have a constancy of purpose in my position. Our organization has developed a constancy of purpose.	____	___	____
6. It is my policy and the policy of this organization to fix the process rather than to fix blame.	____	___	____
7. We emphasize teamwork and cooperation in our school and district.	____	___	____
8. Everyone in this organization works to build trust and respect.	____	___	____
9. Our organization focuses on using data to make decisions.	____	___	____
10. When problems occur, we focus on correcting the process and not on blaming the person.	____	___	____
11. Our organization focuses on providing all staff with constant education and training.	____	___	____
12. We have implemented the continuous improvement cycle in this organization.	____	___	____
13. We work to meet our customer's requirements the first time and every time.	____	___	____
14. We use quality tools and techniques to analyze and solve our problems.	____	___	____
15. In this organization, we practice shared beliefs and values.	____	___	____
16. Our organization has developed vision and mission statements.	____	___	____
17. As a member of the staff, I support the vision and mission adopted by this organization.	____	___	____

Principles	#1	#2	#3
18. As an individual and as an organization, we are committed to systemic planning. We consider the effect our decisions will have on all of the functional groups of the entire organization.	___	___	___
19. All stakeholder groups are involved in the decision process for our organization.	___	___	___
20. The value of the products and services we provide our customers is clearly evident to all stakeholder groups.	___	___	___
TOTALS	___	___	___

To determine the Phase of Quality, total the number of points for each individual and determine the appropriate phase in which he or she should be placed. At the conclusion of the survey analysis, total the percentages for each phase and map the percentages on a Phases of Quality histogram.

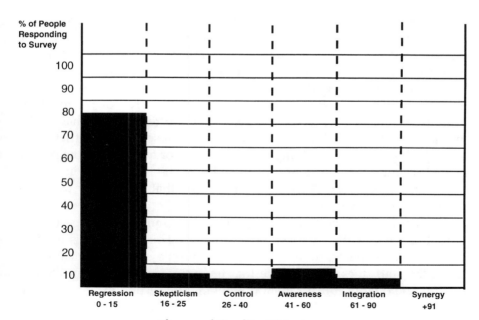

Phases of Quality Histogram

In the preceding example, the dominant phase is regression. People in regression will resist any attempt to get them to change the way they work. If you start your quality transformation with this group of individuals, you will fail. The various phases of quality are defined as follows:

- **Regression:** People refuse to accept the concepts of *quality* and *customer.*

- **Skepticism:** People accept the concepts of *quality* and *customer* but need to be convinced of their applicability to education.

- **Control:** This is a very dangerous stage. People in this stage have tried to adopt a different way of doing their work. However, they feel that they are losing control of their environment.

- **Awareness:** People support the concepts of quality. They want to be part of the quality transformation.

- **Integration:** This is a fun stage. This group is quality driven. Everything done is done in a quality manner.

- **Synergy:** In this stage, suppliers, producers, and customers are one. They are a team.

The survey can also be used to determine group or team attitudes toward the principles of quality. To determine the Phase of Quality for a group or team, total the number of points for each individual in the group and plot the results on a Phases of Quality histogram.

Fourteen people participated in the Principles of Quality Survey illustrated in the first histogram on the next page. Ten of the fourteen individuals are in the Phases of Quality that are resistant to change. To initiate a quality transformation in the team, the school or district must provide the team with training in the concepts of quality and the school or district must capitalize on the attitudes of the individuals in the integration and synergy phases to demonstrate that the quality transformation benefits everyone.

Another use of the Phases of Quality histogram is to compare individual rankings with organizational rankings. This approach is used to determine staff perceptions of the organization's commitment to quality. If the staff does not perceive that the organization is committed to quality, the quality transformation will fail. The second example on the next page illustrates this use of the Phases of Quality histogram as a comparison tool.

Each box represents an individual response.

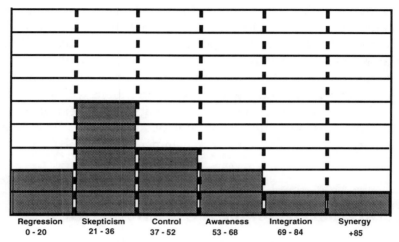

Team Phases of Quality Histogram

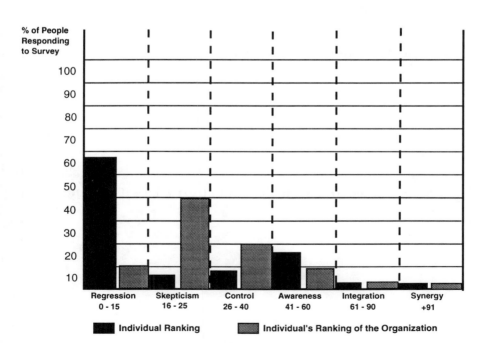

Phases of Quality Histogram

In this example, the staff has a mixed view of the school or district's commitment to quality. The majority of the staff believe that the organization is in the control phase. This reflects the traditional management philosophy that exists in many schools, where all decisions flow down from the top. To correct this perception, the school board and administrators must demonstrate their commitment to quality through their actions. As the quality transformation is reinforced by senior management, the personal and organizational perceptions will become balanced.

This is an appropriate time to use a video to reinforce the quality concepts presented during the previous discussion. "Paradigm Shift," by Joel Barker of Visioning, is recommended.

EXERCISE: DESCRIBE A QUALITY SCHOOL

You have begun to think about what quality in education means. In this activity, you have the opportunity to imagine what a Total Quality School would look like.

Develop a definition of a Total Quality School.

Describe the environment that would exist in a Total Quality School.

DR. W. EDWARDS DEMING'S
QUALITY PRINCIPLES APPLIED TO EDUCATION

Dr. W. Edwards Deming developed Fourteen Points that describe what is necessary for a business to develop a quality culture. Dr. Deming linked his Fourteen Points to the survival of a business. Initially, many educators attempted to apply Dr. Deming's points to education without taking into consideration the unique cultural, political, and legal constraints of education. The following is an adaptation of Dr. Deming's Fourteen Points for education. The quality points were developed by the Amherst School District in Amherst, New Hampshire. They are based on work with Region 3 Technical High School in Lincoln, Maine and Soundwell College in Bristol, England. Schools that have achieved the objectives outlined in these points have improved administrative and student outcomes. These points are called the "Essence of Quality In Education."

1. Create a Constancy of Purpose

Create a constancy of purpose to improve student and service quality, with the aim to become competitive with world-class schools.

2. Adopt a Total Quality Philosophy

Education is in a highly competitive environment and is viewed as one of the major reasons why America is losing its competitive advantage. School systems must welcome the challenge to compete in a global economy. Every member of the education system must learn new skills that support the quality revolution. People must be willing to accept the quality challenge. People must take responsibility for improving the quality of the products or services they provide to their internal and external customers. Everyone must learn to operate more efficiently and productively. Everyone must subscribe to the principles of quality.

3. Reduce the Need for Testing

Reduce the need for testing and inspection on a mass basis by building quality into education services. Provide a learning environment that results in quality student performance.

4. Award School Business in New Ways

Award school business in ways which minimize the total cost to education. Think of schools as suppliers of students from one grade level to the next. Work with parents and agencies to improve the quality of students coming into the system.

5. Improve Quality and Productivity and Reduce Costs

Improve quality and productivity, and thus reduce costs, by instituting a "Chart-It/Check-It/Change-It" process. Describe the process to be improved, identify the customer/supplier chain, identify areas for improvement; implement the changes, assess and measure the results, and document and standardize the process. Start the cycle over again to achieve an even higher standard.

6. Lifelong Learning

Quality begins and ends with training. If you expect people to change the way they do things, you must provide them with the tools necessary to change their work processes. Training provides people with the tools necessary to improve their work processes.

7. Leadership in Education

It is management's responsibility to provide direction. Managers in education must develop a vision and mission statement for the district, school, or department. The vision and mission must be shared and supported by the teachers, staff, students, parents, and community. Quality must be incorporated in the vision and mission statements. Finally, management must "walk-the-talk." Management must preach and practice the quality principles.

8. Eliminate Fear

Drive fear out of the district, school, or department so that everyone works effectively for school improvement. Create an environment that encourages people to speak freely. Adversarial relationships are out-moded and counterproductive.

9. Eliminate the Barriers to Success

Management is responsible for breaking down barriers that prevent people from succeeding in their work. Break down barriers between departments. People in teaching, special education, accounting, food services, administration, curriculum development, research, and other groups must work as a team. Develop movement strategies: move from competition with other groups to collaboration; move from a win–lose resolution to a win–win resolution; move from isolated problem solving to shared problem solving; move from guarding information to sharing information; move from resisting change to welcoming change.

10. Create a Quality Culture

Create a quality culture. Do not let the movement become dependent upon any one individual or group of individuals. Creating a quality culture is everyone's responsibility.

11. Process Improvement

No process is ever perfect; therefore, finding a better way, a better process, applies equally and non-judgmentally. Finding solutions takes precedence over finding fault. Recognize people and groups that make the improvements happen.

12. Help Students Succeed

Remove the barriers that rob students, teachers, and administrators of their right to pride of workmanship. People must want to be involved and do their jobs well. The responsibility of all education administrators must be changed from quantity to quality.

13. Commitment

Management must be committed to a quality culture. Management must be willing to support the introduction of new ways of doing things into the education system. Management must back up goals (the ends) by providing the means to achieve those goals or risk generating resentment within the system. "Do it right the first time" is a lofty goal. Employees become frustrated when management does not understand their problems in achieving a goal or does not care enough to find out about them.

14. Responsibility

Put everyone in the school to work to accomplish the quality transformation. The transformation is everyone's job.

CHAPTER 6

EXAMPLES OF
QUALITY SCHOOLS

The following examples will help you develop an understanding of how schools are implementing quality to improve administrative and student outcomes.

BAY-ARENAC INTERMEDIATE SCHOOL DISTRICT

The Bay-Arenac Intermediate School District is located in Bay City, Michigan. Dr. Jon Whan was appointed superintendent of schools in January 1993. One of Dr. Whan's first official acts was to develop a quality initiative for the district. Prior to the district's adoption of the quality initiative, everyone in the district was provided with an overview of quality. Staff reviewed the implementation process and were encouraged to explore alternative school improvement programs. At the end of the awareness session, staff overwhelming adopted the quality initiative.

The Bay-Arenac Intermediate School District has strongly and uniformly embraced the principles of quality. All staff are treated with respect. Staff are encouraged to explore new ways of improving administrative and student outcomes. Staff training is a key priority for the district. The school board and superintendent work together to create an open environment that encourages total participation in the quality initiative. Everyone is viewed as a quality leader, and everyone is encouraged to explore ideas that will help the district achieve its vision. The district has develop a strong quality foundation.

The Bay-Arenac quality initiative is based on the culture of the organization instead of the beliefs of the superintendent or quality driver. (A quality driver is someone who is committed to quality and forces quality into an organization. Once the quality driver leaves the organization, the quality initiative usually fails.) A core planning team was created to manage the quality initiative. Internal quality facilitators were trained to train other staff members and to facilitate cross-functional quality teams. Individual departments are implementing quality to improve the budgeting process, create a positive cultural environment, and develop new products and offerings for the district.

During the summer of 1994, the district conducted its second district-wide Quality Institute. Staff were surveyed to determine their needs, a district-specific curriculum was developed, and support manuals were created. The institute was an overwhelming success. Administrative, teaching, and support staff representatives worked together to solve problems. Teams focused on improving the processes they directly controlled. A follow-up session was conducted during the fall.

However, the Bay-Arenac quality initiative is unique because of the investment that was made in the staff. During the initial year of the initiative, the major goal of the district was to help the staff develop both an internal and an external customer focus. Traditionally, educators understand the basic concept of an external customer. Although they do not call students or parents customers, educators strive to meet every reasonable request of parents. Educators will go to great lengths to help students succeed. However, this same drive for customer satisfaction is not reflected in the way educators treat other educators. The Bay-Arenac district was successful in creating a quality culture because it focused on helping the staff develop a process for improving internal customer satisfaction.

The success of the Bay-Arenac program is due in large part to the efforts of the members of the core planning team and the quality coordinators. The quality coordinators constantly monitored progress of the implementation to ensure that the initiative reflected the district's requirements. All too often, district's place sole responsibility for the success of the initiative on external consultants. The Bay-Arenac district established a win–win relationship with its consultants to ensure the success of the program.

Because of the progress made during the first year of the project, the Bay-Arenac initiative quickly moved forward. Staff have been able to progress at their own pace. Dr. Whan has made a point of working with his staff to remove the barriers that prevent people from being successful, and staff members are encouraged to develop new ways of working to increase productivity and service quality. Because the district's resources are shrinking, staff members are finding new ways to generate revenue. The district's distant learning programs are innovative. The Bay-Arenac Intermediate School District has develop a total customer focus that is helping the school districts in Bay and Arenac to improve the quality of the educational services provided to the communities.

REGION 3 TECHNICAL HIGH SCHOOL

Region 3 Technical High School is located in Lincoln, Maine. The school provides vocational and technical training for five school districts. The school began its quality journey in 1992. The communities served by the high school are dependent upon the local paper mills for their survival. The paper mills have been implementing quality to remain competitive in a highly competitive global market.

The director of the school, Ashley LeBlanc, views quality as a means of establishing a closer relationship with the business community. Quality provides the school with the opportunity to establish a closer relationship with its primary customers, the students. The programs offered by the school are similar to programs offered by other technical and vocational high schools in the state. However, the one thing that sets this school apart from the other technical high schools in Maine is the staff's dedication to quality.

Mr. LeBlanc is a true quality leader. He is actively removing the barriers that prevent the staff and students from achieving success. Mr. LeBlanc is constantly looking for new programs that the school can implement to achieve high customer satisfaction. During the past two years, the administrative office was able to reduce the school's operating expenses by approximately 10% by adopting quality systems that reduce costs.

The school's staff is uniquely prepared to implement quality. Quality is evident from the first time a visitor enters a classroom. Instructors and students have adopted vision and mission statements for the classroom. Students are part of the evaluation process. A code of conduct was developed for the school and for each class. Students are encouraged to manage their learning process, and a student council was created to facilitate the quality transformation process.

The school has a customer focus. But this could not have been accomplished without the support of the school board and the director. This school was one of the first schools in Maine to implement quality. Other schools tried to implement quality but failed. It was not the principles of quality that failed—it was the implementation process. The staff and school board were quality pioneers in education.

Not all staff embraced the quality initiative. However, as student enrollment declined, the staff viewed quality as a way to develop programs that met or exceeded customer requirements. Unlike other schools, the Region 3 Technical High School must recruit students from the communities it serves. Quality was initially used by the staff to define customer requirements and to develop courses that meet or exceed those requirements. The processes implemented by the staff improved the recruitment process.

The school is continuing in its quality journey. It was recently mentioned in an article in the *Wall Street Journal* for its adoption of a vision and mission. The staff and director frequently participate in quality training sessions. Quality has a real meaning for this school. Unlike other school districts in Maine, this district has made its own financial investment in quality. This investment is helping the school to succeed in an environment where state officials believe that technical high schools have outlived their usefulness.

CHAPTER 7

TQM
IMPLEMENTATION WHEEL

The TQM Implementation Wheel depicted on the next page is a process designed to help implement quality in a school or district. By following the steps depicted in the cycle, you can undertake quality improvement efforts that will make a difference in your school or district. The Implementation Wheel provides a step-by-step procedure for implementing quality in every organization in education. The first four steps focus on meeting customer requirements and obtaining support for change within the school system.

The next four steps take you through the selection, implementation, and assessment phases of quality. These steps enable you to assess your work and to develop quality standards for your school or district. Schools can achieve the first four steps but fail to complete the quality cycle. The biggest problem educators seem to face when implementing quality is getting external and internal customers to agree on process requirements. This breakdown in the customer/supplier chain contributes to the inability of schools to accurately determine what is expected of them.

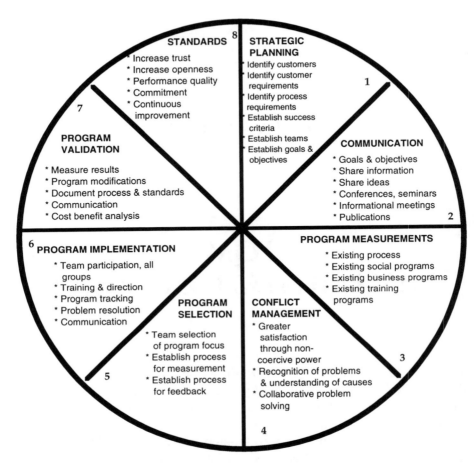

STANDARDS 8
* Increase trust
* Increase openness
* Performance quality
* Commitment
* Continuous improvement

7

PROGRAM VALIDATION
* Measure results
* Program modifications
* Document process & standards
* Communication
* Cost benefit analysis

STRATEGIC PLANNING
* Identify customers
* Identify customer requirements
* Identify process requirements
* Establish success criteria
* Establish teams
* Establish goals & objectives

1

COMMUNICATION
* Goals & objectives
* Share information
* Share ideas
* Conferences, seminars
* Informational meetings
* Publications

2

6 **PROGRAM IMPLEMENTATION**
* Team participation, all groups
* Training & direction
* Program tracking
* Problem resolution
* Communication

PROGRAM SELECTION
* Team selection of program focus
* Establish process for measurement
* Establish process for feedback

5

PROGRAM MEASUREMENTS
* Existing process
* Existing social programs
* Existing business programs
* Existing training programs

CONFLICT MANAGEMENT
* Greater satisfaction through non-coercive power
* Recognition of problems & understanding of causes
* Collaborative problem solving

3

4

Total Quality Management Cycle for Education

CHAPTER 8

ORGANIZING
FOR QUALITY

In this chapter, we will discuss the support systems that are required for quality to be successfully implemented in a school or district. We will also review the process for planting the seeds of quality in a school or district to gain broad support for the quality transformation. Once the concepts of quality have been accepted in a school or district, the work of the Initial Planning Committee is complete and the Quality Steering Committee guides the implementation of quality on a departmental, school-wide, and/or district-wide basis.

The Organizing for Quality phase focuses on the organizational structure that schools must develop in order to successfully implement quality-focused project teams. The discussion in this chapter is centered around the creation of district-wide or school-wide Initial Planning Teams and Quality Steering Committees. The Initial Planning Team is the vehicle that schools and school districts use to prepare the education environment and the community for the quality transformation. The Quality Steering Committee guides the quality transformation throughout the school or district.

The Quality Steering Committee establishes the guidelines for the creation of Quality Task Teams. Quality Task Teams implement quality tools and techniques to improve specific administrative, staff, and student outcomes. Generally, Quality Task Teams are cross-functional teams that address school-wide or district-wide issues. In this section, we will also discuss the process for identifying the members of cross-functional Quality Task Teams. Quality principles for the organizational structure of such teams will be suggested, and the quality principles by which the Quality Task Teams conduct their meetings will be reviewed.

The techniques outlined in this chapter will enable you to build a strong foundation for your quality initiative. The creation of a strong foundation will enable your school or district's quality transformation to become culture dependent rather than person dependent. A strong foundation provides the quality movement with the resources required to complete the cultural transformation that is necessary for success.

The following implementation schedules have been developed for the Organizing for Quality phase. The schedules identify the tasks that must be completed during each phase and the sequence for initiating the various tasks. As you will note, several tasks may be carried out simultaneously, and each task builds on the experience gained from the previous task.

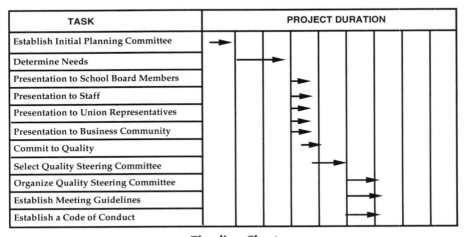

Timeline Chart

A considerable number of recent articles describe the implementation of quality. In many instances, the information presented in such articles conflicts with the actual process. Our goal here is to provide you with a realistic time frame in which you can plan your quality activities. In reality, your time frame will differ from the one outlined above.

The introduction of quality in education begins with the establishment of an Initial Planning Committee. The role of this committee is to guide the project through the organizational phases. It is recommended that membership on the committee be limited to no more than five individuals. Usually, the superintendent or assistant superintendent of schools is the chairperson of the committee. Other members on the committee generally include a member of the school board, a teacher, an administrator, and a support staff representative. Once the Quality Steering Committee has been established, the role of the Initial Planning Committee is completed, but the Initial Planning Committee generally becomes part of the Steering Committee to handle day-to-day issues.

The major danger schools encounter in establishing the Initial Planning Committee is selecting representatives solely from senior management. This structure will make it difficult for the team to generate broad support for the program. In 1991, Soundwell College in Bristol, England established a Quality Planning Committee to explore ways in which quality could be introduced into the college. The Quality Planning Committee was comprised of representatives from the Senior Management Team. The staff in the college viewed the program as a management program and resisted the team's efforts to introduce quality on a college-wide basis. For the team to be successful, everyone in the organization must support the team's efforts.

APPLYING YOUR KNOWLEDGE: EXERCISE

Building the Initial Planning Committee

In this exercise, you will establish the Initial Planning Committee for your school or district. The focus of the exercise is to help you determine the qualifications for the individuals that you would like to serve on this committee. You will invite the people you select to serve on the committee.

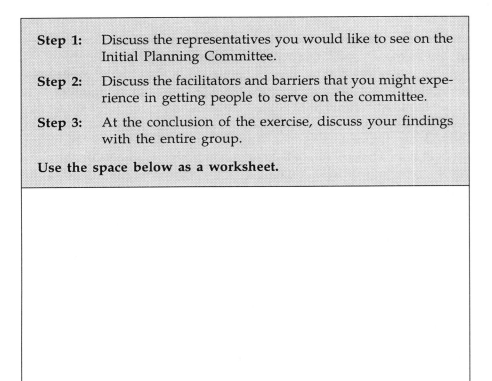

Step 1: Discuss the representatives you would like to see on the Initial Planning Committee.

Step 2: Discuss the facilitators and barriers that you might experience in getting people to serve on the committee.

Step 3: At the conclusion of the exercise, discuss your findings with the entire group.

Use the space below as a worksheet.

DETERMINING THE REQUIREMENTS FOR SUCCESS

One of the major functions of the Initial Planning Committee is to establish the fact that there is a need to change the way things are being done. This may seem like a trivial matter. We all know that we must improve the quality of education. However, if you talk to people in education, they will tell you that they are doing a quality job and the problem lies with society and not with education. Data must be collected to demonstrate to the staff and the community that there are areas where the quality of education can be improved. The collection of data removes the project from the abstract and makes it an issue to which people can relate.

For example, Region 3 Technical High School in Lincoln, Maine conducted a detailed needs analysis to determine those areas of education that could be improved and to gauge community support for the school's quality effort. The Planning Committee sent surveys and questionnaires to every student who had graduated from the school within the past five years. The students were asked to rate the quality of the education they received. Graduates were asked if they were using the skills they were taught at Region 3 Technical High School and were asked if they would recommend the school to potential students. To the staff's amazement, very few of the graduates were using the skills they had learned at Region 3 Technical High School in their careers.

The committee also contacted businesses in the area and representatives of local government. The businesses were asked if they were aware of the programs provided at Region 3 Technical High School. They were also asked if they employed any graduates from the school and to rank their experiences with these employees on a scale of 1 to 5 (5 being the highest). Representatives of government were asked if they had ever visited Region 3 Technical High School. They were asked to rank the quality of education provided at the school. Government representatives were also asked if they thought the school was providing them with value for the money received from the community.

Finally, the committee contacted current and future students to determine their perceptions of the school. Current students were asked to rate the quality of the programs provided at the school. Potential students were asked to discuss what would attract them to the school. Parents of current students were asked if they were aware of the programs offered by the school and to rate the quality of education their children received at the school.

The team collated the information and prepared a quality profile for the school. The team was shocked to learn that many representatives of the business community were not aware of the programs offered at Region 3 Technical High School. Representatives of the business community also expressed their concern that graduates of the school were not prepared to enter the labor market. This concern was reinforced by the fact that very few graduates of the school were actually working in the career fields they had studied in school. The representatives from government found it difficult to determine the school's added value. Responses from current and potential students indicated that enrollment was going to decline. Obviously, the school's current programs did not meet the students' requirements.

This information was presented to the entire staff of the school. The staff reviewed the information and discussed it at several meetings. Staff members began to question their teaching capabilities and, to his credit, the director of the school, Mr. Ashley LeBlanc, told the staff that they were not at fault. Mr. LeBlanc focused on helping the staff to identify and correct the systems problems that were preventing them from doing a good job. At the conclusion of this process, everyone was committed to implementing quality in the school.

APPLYING YOUR KNOWLEDGE: EXERCISE

Developing a Quality Focus

In this exercise, you will determine what data you will need to collect to establish your quality foundation. The data you collect will help you to focus your school and district's efforts on improving the quality of every educational process. The data will also be used to help you build an alliance between education, business, and government.

Step 1: Discuss the kind of information that you believe people in your school or district and community would require before they would consider supporting a quality program.

Step 2: Develop a sample questionnaire that your school or district might use to collect the data required. Determine how the information will be collected.

Step 3: Discuss your team's output with the entire group.

Use the space below as a worksheet.

PRESENTATION TO THE SCHOOL BOARD

The Initial Planning Committee must present its findings to the school board and representatives of the community. At Region 3 Technical High School, the Planning Committee used this presentation as an opportunity to build broad support for its program. School board members were pleased that the staff would explore ways to improve the quality of education. Representatives from the community never realized the pride and dedication of the staff at the school. The committee gained community-wide support for its quality program. One of the major messages received from the business community was that the school could not afford not to implement quality. If the school expected its graduates to be prepared to enter the work force, then the school had to modify its curriculum to meet current labor market requirements.

QUALITY STEERING COMMITTEE

The Quality Steering Committee, or Core Planning Team as it is called in several districts, is created after the Initial Planning Team has completed all of its activities. All of the stakeholders of education should be represented on the Quality Steering Committee. Initially, the Steering Committee may be comprised of members of the school board, teaching staff, administrators, and support staff. As the program expands, the composition of the committee should be expanded to include government representatives, business and community leaders, parents, and students.

The timeline chart on the next page depicts the schedule for creating the Quality Steering Committee.

The Steering Committee helps to establish an alliance between education, business, and government. It promotes greater participation in the education process by students and parents. The committee provides direction and resources for the quality teams. Above all, the committee prevents any one individual or group of individuals from sabotaging the program.

Quality forces people to do things in a different way. Unfortunately, some people cannot change and others simply do not want to change. These people will do everything in their power to destroy the new

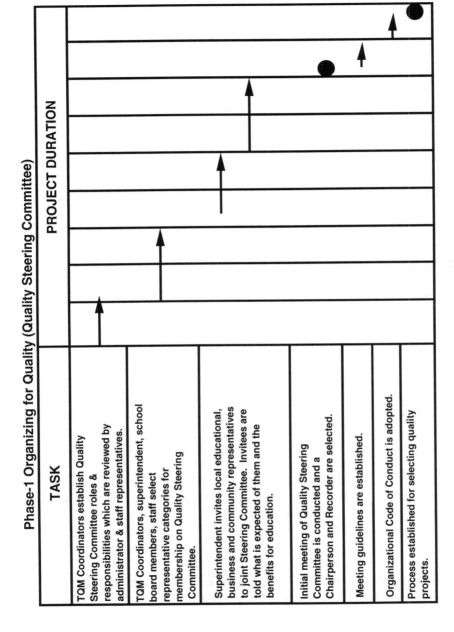

Phase-1 Organizing for Quality (Quality Steering Committee)

PROJECT DURATION

TASK
TQM Coordinators establish Quality Steering Committee roles & responsibilities which are reviewed by administrator & staff representatives.
TQM Coordinators, superintendent, school board members, staff select representative categories for membership on Quality Steering Committee.
Superintendent invites local educational, business and community representatives to joint Steering Committee. Invitees are told what is expected of them and the benefits for education.
Initial meeting of Quality Steering Committee is conducted and a Chairperson and Recorder are selected.
Meeting guidelines are established.
Organizational Code of Conduct is adopted.
Process established for selecting quality projects.

Timeline Chart

program. The Steering Committee prevents these people from getting their way.

In one district in northern Maine, the director of a school became ill and was absent from the school for approximately six weeks. During that period of time, one of the instructors threatened the other TQM facilitators in the program and did everything in his power to prevent the program from going forward. The behavior of this individual was brought to the attention of the Steering Committee. The Steering Committee supported the majority of the staff in their efforts to develop a quality school. Once the individual found out that he did not have a platform from which to promote his cause, he blended into the program. Has this individual adopted a quality philosophy? Probably not. However, a quality initiative cannot succeed unless it has the support of a school-wide or district-wide Steering Committee.

The following are suggested guidelines for the organization of a Quality Steering Committee.

Facilitator

Many education professionals indicate that they do not need a facilitator to manage their team meetings. They are professionals who know how to research and solve problems. Unfortunately, we all join a team with certain biases. Subconsciously, we try to manage and direct the process. This subconscious power struggle for dominance can sabotage the team process. A TQM facilitator is someone who has an objective view of the problem. It is the facilitator's job to keep the team focused on the task at hand. The facilitator should possess good people skills and should have a detailed understanding of the use and application of TQM tools and techniques. All too often, teams struggle through issues that could easily be resolved if a facilitator were managing the team meetings. The facilitator must understand TQM. This cannot be an on-the-job learning experience. If it is, the team will fail.

Team Leader

The team leader should be selected by the group at the initial team meeting. The facilitator should manage the process for selecting the team leader. Usually, the team members vote on the team leader. A common problem is that the most popular person in the group often becomes the team leader. It is important to avoid this selection method because this individual may not be the best person to direct the team. The team leader must have good leadership skills and should have successfully led other teams. He or she should have experience in implementing quality tools and techniques. The team leader has something to gain by fixing the problem.

Team Recorder

The comment most frequently heard from schools is that the quality team did an excellent job solving the problem, but did not have the time to document what they did. A major function of a quality team is to develop an experience base that can be shared with other members of the school or district. Therefore, every team should select someone to serve as team recorder. It is the responsibility of the team recorder to keep minutes of the meetings, publish an agenda for all meetings, and document how the team solved the problem, the tools that were used, the problems that were encountered, and the benefits derived for the district, school, students, staff, and community.

APPLYING YOUR KNOWLEDGE: EXERCISE

Establishing Your Steering Committee

In this exercise, you will select the people you would like to serve on the Steering Committee. You may decide that some of the members, such as representatives from the teaching staff, will be elected by the group to serve on the committee. Determine the representatives who must serve on the committee and the process by which they should be appointed to the committee.

Step 1: Identify the representatives you believe should serve on the school-wide or district-wide Steering Committee.

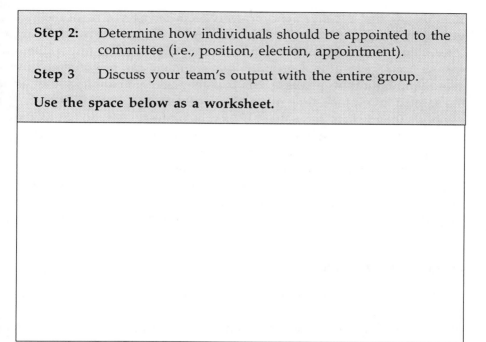

Step 2: Determine how individuals should be appointed to the committee (i.e., position, election, appointment).

Step 3 Discuss your team's output with the entire group.

Use the space below as a worksheet.

QUALITY STEERING COMMITTEE MEETING GUIDELINES

Every team should establish ground rules which will govern the team's activities and meetings. One of the major causes of failure in implementing quality is the inability of people on a team to build trust among the team members. Quality teams should build partnerships between themselves and all of the stakeholders of the process. As the level of trust increases among the team members and between the team and the stakeholders, the team will create better learning and working environments. The following are successful hints for managing team meetings.

Meeting Location

Schedule a convenient meeting location. Make sure that the location is reserved well in advance of the meeting. Establish a date and time for the meeting that is convenient for every team member. One of the biggest complaints in education is that meetings have to be scheduled during after-school hours. Members want to know who is going to pay them for the time they put in. Generally, this argument can be countered by reminding education professionals that they are professionals and, as such, must invest their time in creating a professional environment that supports their beliefs and values. If they, as professionals, do not fix the problem, someone else will—and they may not like the solution. When this argument is raised, participants can be asked to list what it means to them as individuals and to the students, district, and school for them to solve this problem. At the end of this exercise, all of the comments are combined on a flip chart. Generally, the list of benefits becomes so long that everyone recognizes the value of solving the problem.

Meeting Attendance

Meeting attendance is mandatory, although there may be a legitimate reason why someone cannot attend a meeting. When someone cannot attend a meeting, he or she must notify the team leader. When someone misses a meeting, he or she agrees to accept any task assigned by the team. If someone consistently misses meetings, he or she should be asked to resign from the team and a replacement should be selected.

Promptness and Attention

Each meeting should start and end on time. The participants should give the meeting their full attention. They should not be working on another task while at the meeting. Phone calls should not be allowed except for emergencies. Distractions should be kept to a minimum. Break periods should be established at the beginning of the meeting.

Agenda and Minutes

The team should agree on the agenda for the next meeting prior to the conclusion of each meeting. The team recorder should keep minutes of each meeting. The minutes of the previous meeting and the agenda for the next meeting should be sent to the team members in advance of each meeting. The minutes should reflect the tasks that have been assigned to individual members. The team recorder should keep a central file of the minutes of team meetings. The central file should also contain the project reports submitted by each team member as projects are concluded.

Roles and Responsibilities

Generally, the team will assign specific tasks to team members. However, there may be regular duties that the team may assign to one or two members. These tasks should be assigned to members at the initial meeting. For example, team meetings in England require afternoon tea. One person is assigned responsibility for ensuring that tea is available for the members.

Team Skill Assessment

Early in the problem-solving process, the team should determine the areas of expertise for each member of the team. This will enable the team to identify the external resource requirements that may be needed to solve problems. For example, at one high school that is developing an economic resource database for the community, the team is comprised of representatives from the school, the chamber of commerce, the community, and the student population. The team developed a list of expertise for each member of the team and realized that they lacked a member with expertise in computer skills. External resources had to be secured to complete the task.

Resource Requirements

This is a major issue that is often overlooked. Very early in the problem-solving process, the team should develop a list of resources that will be needed to resolve the problem. One of the key roles of the Quality Steering Committee is to provide the improvement teams with the resources they will need to do their job. A major complaint heard from improvement teams is that the Steering Committee does not respond to their requests for assistance in a timely manner. Steering Committees complain that they are not provided with sufficient notification from the improvement teams as to the resources required.

Project Schedule

Every team should establish a project schedule prior to beginning work. This will enable the team members to schedule team meetings in their calendars. It will help management to understand the processes the team will use to the solve the problem. It provides the team with specific milestones and objectives by which it can measure its progress. Developing a project schedule helps the team to be efficient and eliminate wasted effort.

Communication

The team should establish a process by which it can communicate its work to others. Team communications should summarize the team's activities. Other members of the school or district will thus be kept informed of the team's activities and, in many instances, can provide valuable comments to the team. It is important for the team to remember to summarize its activities in a general report. Focus on providing others with important information. Whenever possible, use existing communication processes to keep others informed.

APPLYING YOUR KNOWLEDGE: EXERCISE

Establishing Team Meeting Processes and Procedures

In this exercise, you will establish the processes and procedures that your quality teams will use. An agreed-upon format will prevent groups from developing conflicting guidelines and will ensure that no one individual or group dominates the quality transformation.

Step 1: Identify the characteristics of an effective team and the guidelines by which that team would operate.

Step 2: Develop the guidelines for your quality teams. Remember, each school has a unique culture and some guidelines may not be appropriate for certain schools.

Step 3: Discuss your team's output with the entire group.

Use the space below as a worksheet.

CHAPTER 9

CREATING QUALITY TASK TEAMS

A Quality Task Team is a team created to solve a problem that cannot easily be solved by an employee and his or her supervisor during the normal course of business activity. There are two types of Quality Task Teams: cross-functional task teams and departmental task teams. A cross-functional task team is usually created by the Quality Steering Committee to solve district-wide or school-wide problems. The cross-functional task team is comprised of staff members from all of the departments impacted by the problem. Departmental task teams focus on departmental problems. Membership on departmental task teams is usually limited to departmental staff. Generally, the Quality Steering Committee or Core Planning Team does not monitor or manage the activities of departmental task teams.

Task teams should be organized to address problems that have a significant impact on the school or district. These problems should be recurring problems, and resolution of the problem should significantly improve the educational process.

The problems addressed by task teams are of such a nature that they require team members with different kinds of expertise to solve. Because the team's resources are limited, one of the principal responsibilities of the task team is to prioritize problems in terms of impact, cost reliability, safety, environmental factors, and ease of solution. The team must determine which area it will address first. This should be the area that will have the greatest impact on improving the outcome.

All of the stakeholders of the process must be represented on Quality Task Teams. Initially, the task teams are comprised of members of the stakeholder groups currently involved in the process. The timeline chart on the next page illustrates how a task team develops its structure to solve the problem.

The processes discussed in the previous chapters were developed over a five-year period of time. They were developed with the cooperation of hundreds of schools in both the United States and Europe. Implementing quality is a big risk for education professionals. It is a risk because people naturally tend to resist change. They become accustomed to the way they work and do not want anyone changing their work processes, even if the change is for the better. The implementation structure presented in this book is designed to help you overcome the barriers to success and will ensure that your quality transformation is an organization-wide transformation.

APPLYING YOUR KNOWLEDGE: EXERCISE

Creating Quality Task Teams

In this exercise, you will create a Quality Task Team for your school or district. List all of the problems impacting your school or district. Select one problem from the list.

Step 1: Identify all of the groups that are impacted by the problem.

Step 2: Select a representative from each group to serve on the task team. (People generally volunteer for the team.)

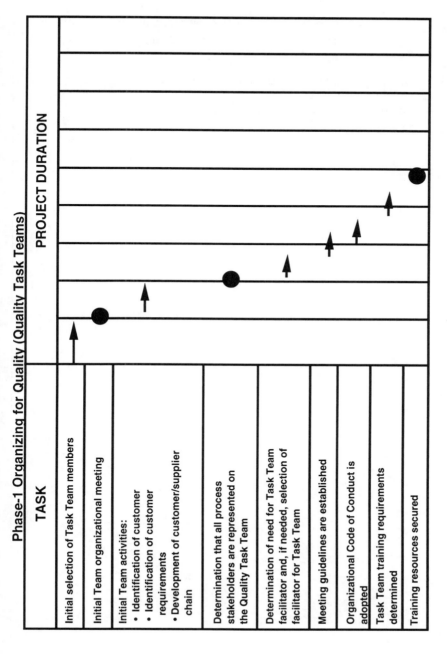

Phase-1 Organizing for Quality (Quality Task Teams)

Timeline Chart

Step 3: Ask the team to define the problem in terms of impact, cost reliability, safety, environmental factors, and ease of solution.

Step 4: Ask the team to identify which area it will focus on first.

Use the space below as a worksheet.

CHAPTER 10

THE PROBLEM-SOLVING CYCLE

The education environment is very complex and, therefore, requires a systematic approach to problem solving. Unlike the problem-solving model for business developed by Dr. W. Edwards Deming (Plan-Do-Check-Act), the problem-solving process for education must follow a logical sequence. The following graphic illustrates the problem-solving cycle for education:

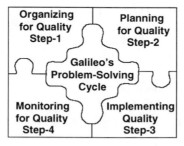

Problem-Solving Cycle for Education

The problem-solving cycle for education must be entered in the Organizing for Quality phase. This is unlike the problem-solving cycle for business, depicted on the next page, which can be entered at any phase.

The problem-solving cycle for education is designed to eliminate a major problem experienced by many schools: the creation of too many task teams. This is a major problem that schools must face and it can significantly increase the cost of implementing quality.

Dr. Deming's Problem-Solving Cycle for Business

For example, recently a superintendent of schools in a midwestern city inquired about the availability of software that could track the progress and membership of task teams. The district has a student population of approximately 7200 students. The superintendent was asked how many task teams had been created. He replied that no one knew the exact number of task teams but that it was in excess of 150. The school board was upset because the parents were complaining about the amount of time teachers were spending out of the classroom.

ORGANIZING FOR QUALITY

The Organizing for Quality phase enables the school to monitor and track the membership and activities of existing quality teams.

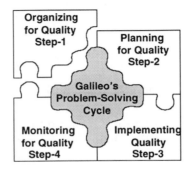

During this phase, the Quality Steering Committee determines that there is a need to create a task team and tracks the number of teams created and the people assigned to each team. This prevents the district or school from creating more teams than can be properly managed, and it prevents people from over-committing themselves to participate in task team activities.

The Quality Steering Committee completes the Organizing for Quality worksheet (see next page) to determine if there is a need to create a task team to solve the problem. This form is easy to use, and it provides direction for the Quality Steering Committee. Department leaders can also use the form to determine if there is a need to create a task team to solve a department-specific problem. If a task team is created, a copy of the form is forwarded to the task team. This form and the forms discussed later in this chapter enable educators to document the action taken and the benefits for the school or district.

PLANNING FOR QUALITY

The next phase in the problem-solving cycle for education is Planning for Quality.

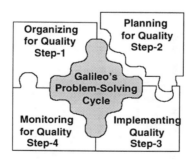

The Planning for Quality phase helps the school or district ensure that all of the stakeholders are involved in the problem-solving process and that the team is solving the correct problem. How many times have you solved a problem in your school or district only to later find out that your solution created additional problems? In the Planning for Quality phase, the district establishes the structure that prevents this problem for occurring.

The steps taken by the team during this phase are outlined in the

Action

List the three most important benefits for the school or district, staff, students and community for solving these issues. Be specific in your description.

Complete all the Action Steps for the Highlighted Question

What are you going to do?	Who is going to do it?	When is it going to be done?	How is it going to be done?

Why are you doing this?

Points to Consider:

- Why have you selected this project?

- Is it to improve your effectiveness as a school or district?

- Is it for prestige and public relations?

- Is it in response to customer complaints?

- What do you hope to achieve?

- Do you know where you are now and where you want to be in your approach to solving the problem?

- List the other problems you plan on addressing?

- What benefits will you gain?

List the Key Points School or District:

Tip:

- If you are doing this for public relations alone, think again. Do you have the commitment that is needed? If not, this is likely to cause the program to fail.

Organizing for Quality Worksheet

following flowchart. The Quality Task Team implements three easy steps to ensure that the right problem is being addressed and that all of the groups that should be part of the problem-solving team are on the team.

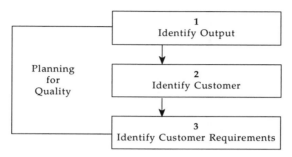

Planning for Quality Flowchart

This process is extremely easy to implement. The task team uses the Planning for Quality worksheet (see next page) to determine what is going to be accomplished. Again, the process has been simplified by providing a worksheet that the team can use to clearly identify requirements that the output must meet. For example, during the development of a learning video for the Richmond County School Board, over two hours of instruction was videotaped. The board's requirements were:

- A videotape of no more than three minutes in length

- A facilitator manual to accompany the video

- Clear and concise instructions for the user

- Follow-up procedures to determine the benefits of the video

All of these requirements were listed on the following form, which enabled creating a video that exceeded the board's expectations. To meet the board's expectations, the length of the video had to be reduced from two hours to three minutes. This was accomplished by narrowing the focus of the video to one tool. A facilitator's manual was developed to provide additional information for the user. The facilitator's manual was simple and easy to use. Finally, a follow-up process was developed which the district could implement to determine the benefits of the video.

In developing the video for the Richmond County Public Schools, the original product specification did not match the board's require-

Complete all the Action Steps for the Highlighted Question

Why are you doing this?	**What are you going to do?**	Who is going to do it?	When is it going to be done?	How is it going to be done?

Points to Consider:

- Who is impacted by this problem?
- Have you clearly defined the problem?
- What are your priorities?
- What approach will the team implement to solve the problem?
- How will they benefit from solving this problem?

Identify the customer and how they will benefit from the resolution of this problem.

Tip: • You may have a great deal to do. Break your work tasks into critical and non-critical tasks. The critical tasks are your major priorities and must be completed first. The non-critical tasks can be assigned to individuals and teams. Evaluation is often a weak point. You will insure your success if you develop an evaluation process in your plan.

Action

Write down the three top priorities and justify the selections.

Identify the customer by name and list them below.

Create a list of the customer's requirements.

Planning for Quality Worksheet

ments. The processes discussed in this phase enabled the development of a product that not only met the board's requirements but also created a marketable product for national distribution.

IMPLEMENTING QUALITY

The next phase in the problem-solving cycle for education is the Implementing Quality phase. During this phase, the team actually solves the problem. This is the most popular phase in the problem-solving cycle.

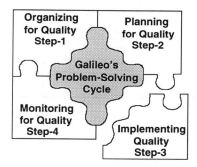

This phase is divided into four steps: how the team will solve the problem, when is it going to be done, how is it going to be done, and the action plan.

The following chart illustrates the steps in the first part of the Implementing Quality phase of the problem-solving cycle. This first step is a simple three-part process that any team can follow to make sure that the right problem has been identified and to develop a potential solution that complies with the constraints established by the school or district and also meets the customer's requirements.

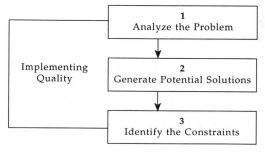

Implementing Quality

Complete all the Action Steps for the Highlighted Question

Why are you doing this?	What are you going to do?	**How will the team solve the problem?**	When is it going to be done?	How is it going to be done?

Points to Consider:

The key points of the problem-solving process are:

- Analyze the Problem

1. List the reasons or factors preventing the desired state from being achieved.
2. Identify the key causes or reasons that prevent the desired state from being achieved.
3. Document and rank the key causes or reasons that prevent the desired state from being achieved.
4. Determine the root causes that prevent the desired state from being achieved.

- Generate Potential Solutions

1. Develop and clarify potential solutions.
2. Rank order the solutions.
3. Determine what needs to change (roles, responsibilities, resources, procedures, policies, communication, structure, etc.)
4. Analyze the forces for and against the proposed solutions.
5. Identify any other stakeholders who need to be involved in the process.

- Identify the Constraints

1. List the constraints that the team must comply with to solve the problem (money, time, resources, facility, etc.)
2. Determine if the team has the authority to make the changes.

Tip: • Ensure that the team has considered all of the potential solutions and that the solution selected can be implemented within the constraints governing the task team.

Action

Write down the key reasons causing the problem.

Write down the potential solutions and rank them.

List the constraints that govern this project.

Implementing Quality Phase

During this step, the problem is analyzed to determine the root causes that are preventing the process from producing the ideal output. Potential solutions are generated, and the solutions are prioritized to select the one that will provide the greatest benefit for the customer.

The team identifies the constraints that govern the project to ensure that the solution meets both the customer's and school or district's requirements. For example, in the problem previously discussed, the financial constraints were the major constraints governing the project. A very complex and entertaining video could have been produced, but the associated costs for this type of instructional video would have far exceeded the customer's financial capability. Therefore, the production process was customized in order to minimize the cost.

Once the initial step has been completed, the team will decide how the solution will be implemented. The Implementing Quality worksheet (see next page) outlines the next step in the Implementing Quality phase of the problem-solving cycle.

During this step, the team will create a timeline to specify when each task will be completed. The team outlines the steps it will take to resolve the problem and identifies the milestones for each phase of the implementation. Once this step is completed, the team is ready to describe how the problem is going to be solved.

In the next step in the Implementing Quality phase of the problem-solving cycle, the team identifies the resources that are needed to correct the problem. This too is an area that is oftentimes overlooked by teams and is the major cause of failure.

There are numerous examples of task teams that failed because they did not have the resources or expertise necessary to implement their solutions. For example, the staff at one school district in southern Maine determined that the most logical and successful way to encourage teachers to participate in the school improvement program was to pay them. This was a great solution, but the district did not have the funds in its budget to pay the teachers for this activity. The administration advised the task team that it could not implement its solution, and the team refused to continue to work on the problem. Budget resources should have been provided to the team, which would have enabled the team to understand the implications caused by the solution.

The final step in the Implementing Quality phase of the problem-solving cycle is the creation of an action plan. In this step, the team transfers the information from the worksheets previously completed to

Complete all the Action Steps for the Highlighted Question

Why are you doing this?	What are you going to do?	Who is going to do it?	**When is it going to be done?**	How is it going to be done?

Points to Consider:

- Can you establish a date when you might be in a position to demonstrate the improvements made?

- What are the milestone that you have established for your projects?

- What task will you work on first?

List the tasks you are working on?

Action

Write down when you aim to achieve:

- **Describe your first significant steps toward quality.**
- **You are your top three priorities?**
- **How will you recognize the contributors?**

Create a Timeline Chart for your task

Tip:

- Make your timetable realistic. Cultural changes always take time to achieve. Do not rush the process.

Implementing Quality Worksheet

**Complete all the Action Steps
for the Highlighted Question**

Why are you doing this?	What are you going to do?	Who is going to do it?	When is it going to be done?	How is it going to be done?

Action

Define the three most important barriers which could prevent you from achieving your quality goals. Describe how you will over come these barriers.

Points to Consider:

• Do you have the resources necessary to complete the tasks?

• Do you have the expertise on-house.

• If not, where can you get?

• What links does your quality transformation have with other school initiatives?

• What is your approach to involving people at all levels in the school, district or your group in the process?

List the Resources Required

Describe how you will obtain the external expertise required for the task.

Tip:

• From links with other schools who are working toward quality. Be honest and realistic in addressing the barriers which you will need to overcome.

Implementing Quality: Resource Requirements

Project Timeline

List the steps to be completed, the date they will be completed by, the milestones by which the project's progress will be measured and the person responsible for the task.

Project Leader: _____

Start Date: _____
End Date: _____

Tasks	Week 1	Week 2	Week 3	Week 4	Week 5	Week 6	Week 7	Week 8

Action Plan
(Provide the Information Requested)

Project: Describe the criterion selected. Explain why you selected this criterion.

Benefits: Described the benefits for the school or district and the external contractor.

Team: List the team members that will work on this project.

Resources: List the resources that will be needed to complete the project. Note if they are internal or external resources. If they are external resources indicate how you will secure them.

Financial Analysis: What are the financial implications to the school or district and the external contractor?

Project Duration: Describe the timeframe for this project.

Project Barriers: List the barriers that you must overcome to be successful. How will you overcome them?

Tips:
Use data to support your observations and assumptions.
Be as specific as you can.
Do not be over aggressive in the selection of a project.
Initially, you should select a project that can be completed within short timeframe.

Action Plan Worksheet for Implementing Quality

an action plan worksheet. This worksheet provides the team with a systematic process to track its progress. It enables the team to make sure that all milestones are achieved and that the project is completed on time. This worksheet also enables the team to clearly identify the roles and responsibilities of team members. It can eliminate many of the causes of conflict that develop within the team and between the team and the rest of the staff in the school or district.

MONITORING FOR QUALITY

In the final phase, the team monitors the results to ensure that the desired results were accomplished.

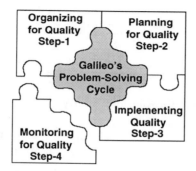

The Monitoring for Quality phase is completely disregarded by business, education, and government organizations. Once a problem has been resolved, the school or district wants to immediately proceed to the next problem. Unfortunately, most schools never verify that the desired results are consistently achieved. This phase in the problem-solving cycle prevents this problem from occurring.

In this phase, the team establishes the quality standards for the solution and uses the Monitoring for Quality worksheet to ensure that the process is producing the desired results. If the process consistently produces the desired result, the team can do one of two things:

- It can be dissolved

- It can implement the continuous improvement cycle

The tasks completed during this phase are illustrated in the following flowchart:

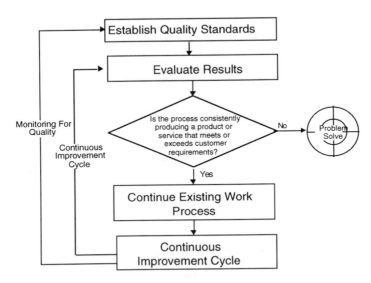

Monitoring for Quality Flowchart

Generally, once the team has completed its work and everyone is satisfied with the quality of the output, the team is dissolved. Before the team completes its work, however, it should document all of its activities and forward the documentation to the Quality Steering Committee. In some instances, the team may decide to further improve the process. This is basis of the continuous improvement cycle. To implement the continuous improvement cycle, the team will raise the quality standard to a higher level. Raising the quality standard can include such things as reducing the time it takes to complete a task, reducing the acceptable number of errors for a function, and reducing the number of people needed to complete a task.

The Monitoring for Quality worksheet (see next page) will help to ensure that your quality teams complete all of the steps in the problem-solving cycle. This will enable you to develop a problem-solving process that provides all staff members with the opportunity to participate in quality teams. It ensures that the correct problem is solved, provides the structure needed to efficiently and effectively solve the problem, and ensures that the desired outcomes are achieved.

Monitoring for Quality

Points to Consider:

- Identify the quality standards for the process.

1. Describe how the process should be performed.
2. List the specific tasks that must be completed

- Evaluate the quality of the output.

1. Does the output consistently meet the customer's requirements?
2. If not, how often does the process fail to produce a quality output?

- Maintain the quality of the output

1. What must be done to maintain the quality of the output?
2. In what order must the tasks be accomplished to maintain the quality of the output?
3. What is needed (supplies) to maintain the quality of the output?
4. What special expertise is needed to produce a quality output?
5. What special resources are needed to maintain the quality of the output?

- Implement the Continuous Improvement Cycle

1. Can the process be further improved?
2. What additional benefits will be realized by the school and students?
3. What will it cost to further improve the quality of the output?
4. What additional resources will be needed to improve the quality of the output?

Describe the action the team will take.

Tip:
- Ensure that all of the stakeholders are involved in the evaluation process. Use project or task teams to tackle the more evaluations.

Action

Write down the key people and organizations who will help to monitor the results.

Identify the quality standards for the process.

Chart (over a predetermined period of time) the quality of the output.

Does the output meet the customer's requirements? If not describe how the team will change the process to produce a quality product.

Monitoring for Quality Worksheet

As outlined on the previous pages, the problem-solving cycle for education can be implemented on a district, school, or departmental basis. The worksheets provide teams with the structure needed to ensure success. The major complaint from educators is that it takes time to complete these forms. But can you afford not to take the time and suffer the cost of failure? Once the staff becomes familiar with the process, it is extremely efficient to implement.

APPLYING YOUR KNOWLEDGE: EXERCISE

Establish a Quality Task Team to Resolve an Issue

In this exercise, you will select the people you would like to serve on the Quality Task Team. You may decide that some of the members, such as representatives from the teaching staff, will be elected to serve on the committee.

Step 1: Follow the model presented in the chapter to identify the output for the process under review.

Step 2: Complete the Organizing for Quality worksheet.

Step 3: Complete the Planning for Quality worksheet.

Step 4: Complete the Implementing Quality worksheets.

Step 5: Complete the Monitoring for Quality worksheet.

Use the space below as a worksheet.

CHAPTER 11

PROBLEM-SOLVING TOOLS AND TECHNIQUES

This chapter introduces the tools needed to analyze and monitor work processes in order to detect problems before they affect the customer/ supplier relationship. Without a work process that functions as expected, efforts to develop customer/supplier partnerships will fail. We must continuously improve the way we work so that we are capable of meeting our customers' challenges and changing needs. One of the major criticisms of education is it has failed to produce an output—students— that meets the changing needs of a global economy. Total Quality Schools are schools that work with their customers and suppliers to ensure that their students are better prepared to meet future business and academic challenges.

In this chapter, we will discuss specific ways of examining your work processes to determine how well they are working and to uncover opportunities for improvement. In the previous chapter, we reviewed ways to clarify and establish customer/supplier requirements. Several tools for evaluating how well those requirements are being met were introduced.

In this chapter, we will review the basic tools of quality. With these tools, you can begin to continuously evaluate and improve your work processes to enhance your customer/supplier relationships.

In Total Quality Schools:

- Every educational process can be improved.

- Every improvement, however big or small, is worthwhile.

- Quality consists of small steps toward improvement, and every effort is recognized for its value.

- Everyone shares responsibility for preventing and fixing problems when they occur.

- Everyone is expected to contribute to the improvement process.

The Problem-Solving Learning Matrix is a guide to the application of quality tools and techniques. Two frequently asked questions are, "In which stage of the quality process is it best to apply tools?" and "Which tools should I use?" If this is your first experience using TQM tools and

Topic	Team Building	Problem Identification	Problem Analysis	Solution Development	Implementation
Vision Statement	●			●	●
Mission Statement	●			●	●
Critical Success Factors	●	●	●	●	●
Flowcharts		●	●	●	●
Process Modeling		●	●	●	●
Cause and Effect Diagram		●	●	●	●
Control Charts		●	●	●	●
Management Assessment	●	●	●	●	●
Staff Assessment	●	●	●	●	●

Problem-Solving Learning Matrix

techniques, you concentrate on using the basic tools of quality. As you become more skilled in the use of TQM tools and techniques, you can include other tools in your problem-solving processes.

TEAM BUILDING

One of the first principles espoused by quality guru Dr. W. Edwards Deming is that there must be a constancy of purpose. Too often, schools operate on the basis of crisis management, which interferes with and takes precedence over planned activities. In addition, personnel turnover on boards and in administration compounds the problem of successful implementation of any programs. As a result, there is no "constancy" and no "purpose" is ever clearly articulated.

The implementation model depicted below helps to ensure "constancy" and articulate "purpose." The model is intended only to pro-

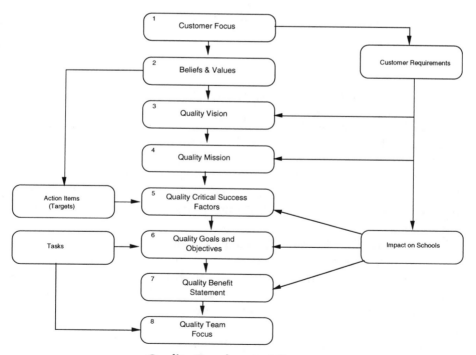

Quality Development Process

vide guidance and examples. It should not be viewed as being set in concrete. Each school district is different; therefore, any improvement effort must be customized to meet the particular circumstances and culture involved. Do not hesitate to make changes as long as the framework and principles remain intact.

In addition to providing constancy and purpose, the model helps to implement the processes required for implementing a continuous improvement effort in schools. The model helps you to:

- Analyze

- Customize

- Qualitize

- Optimize

The implementation model is divided into subprocesses. Each subprocess begins with an explanation of the outcome of that process. This is followed by a description of the specific steps in each process. Where appropriate, each process model will be followed by useful tools and techniques to assist in the process or activity.

DEVELOPING A CUSTOMER FOCUS

A school can collect and utilize data, make effective use of tools and techniques, have a clear understanding of how the work gets done, and implement all the management models and still not be considered an effective organization unless there is a focus on the customer. Many businesses have learned this critical principle of quality the hard way; unfortunately, many others still do not understand the need for a customer focus.

As discussed in Chapter 2, understanding your customer is critical to the quality process. Therefore, it is worthwhile to reinforce the concept of a customer in this chapter. Education is a human service enterprise and, by and large, it has a *captive* customer base. Complicating the issue of customer focus is trying to get agreement as to who the school's customers are.

Once the *internal and external* customers are identified, the next task is trying to meet customer requirements and expectations. In manufacturing a product or providing a service, it is much easier to determine what the customer requires and expects. In education, customer requirements and expectations may be difficult to meet because resources are limited and there is no real consensus as to the specific quality outputs desired and needed.

Nevertheless, if customers are not satisfied (and all such surveys indicate that this is the reality), resources will be difficult to obtain and support will erode; worse yet, changes will be legislated by those who have limited knowledge and understanding of the complexities involved in education.

Who is considered to be a customer? The broadest definition is the person, department, or organizational unit that next receives the value-added product, service, or client. This definition means that at some point in the process, everyone is considered and treated as a customer. In a human enterprise system, such as education, this is a powerful concept because it addresses the reason why cooperation and teamwork are so essential.

Useful Models, Tools, and Techniques

- Surveys and interviews

- Brainstorming

Fourteen Identification Guidelines

1. Identify every group that benefits from the educational enterprise.

2. Identify the internal groups vs. the external groups.

3. Agree on who is(are) the ultimate or primary customer(s).

4. Survey and/or interview the ultimate customer(s) to determine their requirements and expectations.

5. Determine which requirements and expectations are legitimate and reasonable.

6. Analyze the capability of the system to meet the expectations and requirements.

7. If the system does not have the required capability, notify the customers and negotiate what needs to be done.

8. Develop a plan of action with measurable goals and objectives.

9. Communicate the plan to the rest of the school system and other stakeholders.

10. Survey and/or interview the internal customers to determine their requirements and expectations.

11. Determine what is legitimate and reasonable within the context of the requirements and expectations of the external customer(s).

12. Analyze the capability of the system to meet the expectations and requirements.

13. Communicate to the staff what the school can do and how it intends to meet their expectations and requirements.

14. Develop a procedure to ensure that the plans for the external and internal customers are implemented and monitored for success.

BELIEFS AND VALUES

The beliefs and values of the stakeholders must be articulated and a consensus reached. All stakeholders should be involved in the process. Categorizing beliefs and values is an effective way to ensure that all pertinent areas are considered. A list of possible categories is as follows:

- School
- Staff
- Curriculum
- Instruction
- Students
- Parents

- Community

- Customers

- Performance

- Evaluation

Another extremely important quality distinction is that, contrary to the typical list of "we value or believe" statements, each statement must begin with "we are committed to..." **It is one thing to believe something; it is another to make a commitment to make the belief or value a reality.**

Usually, this process begins with the administration and staff and then is reviewed by the school board and eventually all of the stakeholders. This may seem like a long and tedious process, but the values and beliefs must be shared. More importantly, agreement on values and beliefs is the **bond** or **glue** that motivates people to work together, and it forms the foundation upon which to build the continuous improvement process teams.

Useful Models, Tools, and Techniques

- Brainstorming

- Brainwriting

- Customer focus

Examples: Region 3 Technical High School, Lincoln, Maine

*We are committed to providing students
with the learning processes that will enable them
to develop world-class skills in math and science.*

*We are committed to continuous improvement
throughout the organization.*

*We are committed to treating ALL people
with equal respect and values.*

EXERCISE

Use the space below to develop possible belief and value statements for your school or district.

VISION STATEMENT

Developing a vision statement is simply a matter of articulating in no more than one paragraph the desired future state of the school system—something **significantly** better than that which now exists. This vision should be based on the shared values and beliefs.

Again, the process should start with the administration and staff and then reviewed (and changed if necessary) by the governing body and finally all of the stakeholders.

Useful Models, Tools, and Techniques

- Brainstorming
- Brainwriting
- Customer focus

Example: Cape Elizabeth School Department, Cape Elizabeth, Maine

*Success in achieving the Cape's academic mission
will require a deeply committed partnership
among teachers, students, parents and administrators.
This partnership will form, in effect,
a continuous learning organization,
one in which we will hold a stake
and to which we can all contribute.*

EXERCISE

Use the space below to develop a vision statement for your school or district.

MISSION

The purpose of a mission statement is to articulate *how* the vision will be achieved. Developing a mission statement is simply developing a map your school or district will follow to achieve its vision.

Useful Models, Tools, and Techniques

- Brainstorming
- Brainwriting
- Customer focus

Example: Region 3 Technical High School, Lincoln, Maine

It is the mission of
Northern Penobscott Technical High School
to become a Total Quality School,
promoting a continuously improving learning environment
that enhances values, self-esteem, responsibility
and accountability in partnership with
Parents, Business, Education and the Community.

Recommended Action Steps

These are critical steps and ones that will turn the usual rhetoric of values, beliefs, vision, and mission into reality. For *each* value and belief, the administration and staff must address the following in specific, measurable terms:

- What specific activities, procedures, policies, and regulations are already in place that ensure real implementation?
- Which activities, procedures, policies, and regulations (that are in place) need to be changed?
- What measurable new activities, procedures, policies, and regulations need to be implemented during the next 12 months?

These steps accomplish four very important purposes:

1. They represent a way to measure how the beliefs and values are being implemented.
2. They provide a quick and dramatic example that the continuous improvement process is a serious effort.

3. They demonstrate that participation and involvement will be meaningful by providing positive change in everyone's working environment.

4. They will help everyone to realize that they are, in fact, doing many things to honor their commitments.

EXERCISE

Use the space below to develop a mission statement for your school or district.

CRITICAL SUCCESS FACTORS

Critical success factors identify those targets which are critical to the successful achievement of an objective or mission. Critical success factors focus the team's activities on those tasks which are necessary to achieve the desired outcomes.

Five-Step Process

1. The team initially begins by brainstorming all of the possible factors for success. This process is driven by the customer's definition of quality.

2. The team's ideas are then grouped in similar categories. As the groups become smaller, team members begin to realize that there

are a select number of tasks that must be accomplished in order to achieve the desired results.

3. The team proceeds to match the categories to the customer's requirements. The team uses the Critical Success Factor Matrix.

4. The team continues to narrow the list by matching the tasks to the customer's requirements. The team asks, "Does this task achieve the desired result?" A negative response means that the task is eliminated from the list.

5. The final very focused list becomes the team's critical success factors for the project.

Guidelines

1. All of the stakeholders should be involved in the brainstorming session.

2. The team should limit the number of critical success factors. Generally, each project should have no more than eight critical success factors.

The following is an example of a Critical Success Factor Matrix:

CSF / Tasks	Staff Training	Curriculum	Schedule	Classroom Design	Outside Activities	Teacher Delivery	Homework
Communication	●	●	◉	◉	○	●	●
Subject Expertise	●	●	◉	◉	○	●	●
Instructional Design	◉	●	●	●	●	◉	◉
Student Support	○	○	●	●	●	●	●
Individual Learning Skills	○	○	●	○	●	◉	●

Ranking Scale: ● Strong   ◉ Medium   ○ Weak

Critical Success Factor Matrix to Improve Student Grades in Math

---

EXERCISE

Develop a Critical Success Factor Matrix for a process in your school or district.

GOALS AND OBJECTIVES

Goals and objectives are the milestones by which the team can measure its effectiveness. In addition, goals and objectives reflect the team's focus on meeting the customer's requirements. They provide focus and direction for the team and enable the team to evaluate the benefits of the project's outcome. Groups external to the team understand what the team's activities are designed to accomplish. Quality goals and objectives are derived from the critical success factors.

Four-Step Process

1. The team reviews the critical success factors to develop a specific goal for each action item or process. For example, in the Critical Success Factor Matrix on the previous page, one of the critical

success factors is to improve communication. The team's goal is to *develop an effective communication process that provides people with the information they need to do their tasks.*

2. Once the team has developed a goal statement, the team develops a specific action plan for achieving the goal. The action plan contains the steps that must be accomplished. The action steps are the team's objectives. For example, in the case cited above, the team may identify a specific objective such as *delivery of all memos to staff in a timely manner.* The team would establish a specific date by which this is to be accomplished.

3. The team constantly matches its goals and objectives to the customer's requirements. This ensures that the team's activities achieve the results desired by the customer. It also maximizes the use of available resources and minimizes the risk of failure.

4. Goals and objectives also reflect the team's beliefs and values. All too often, the team's beliefs and values conflict with the goals and objectives of the project to which the team was assigned. This always results in failure, and team members become very frustrated with the process. This is the main cause of failure of quality programs. If the team's beliefs and values conflict with the goals and objectives, then the team should stop all activities, and management should develop another focus for the team.

QUALITY BENEFITS STATEMENT

Generally, teams fail to develop a quality benefits statement. Team members and management assume that the customer knows what the benefit of the project is. Unfortunately, this is not the case. In many instances, quality improvement teams set out to improve a process but their outcome does not meet or exceed the customer's requirements. Quality benefits statements are another check in the quality improvement process. The customer can easily determine if the team's efforts are going to be successful. This provides the team with valuable feedback that is necessary to ensure its success. Therefore, quality benefits statements must be closely linked to the customer's requirements.

Quality benefits statements also help your suppliers to understand what you and your customers expect of them. If your suppliers can identify the benefits of their products or services to the ultimate customer, they are more likely to reflect the needs of the ultimate customer in the design of their products and services. Additionally, quality benefits statements can help you to build an alliance between your supplier, your customer, and you.

Example: Avon Advisory Service, Bristol, England

*The Avon Advisory Services provides schools
with management resources critical to their success.*

EXERCISE

Develop a benefits statement for your school, district, or organization.

CHAPTER 12

BASIC
PROBLEM-SOLVING TOOLS

Quality management is founded upon the principle of collecting and using data to define and analyze a problem. Decisions are based on the data. Education leaders can use TQM tools and techniques to collect, analyze, and understand relevant data. However, a word of caution: TQM is **not** tools and techniques. TQM tools and techniques only *assist* in the quality transformation of a school or district. Unfortunately, too many people believe that TQM is tools and techniques—and they are destined for failure.

The matrices illustrated on the following pages depict the typical uses of TQM tools and techniques.

TOOLS:	PROBLEM DEFINITION	PROBLEM ANALYSIS	DATA COLLECTION	DATA ANALYSIS	SOLUTION DEVELOPMENT	SOLUTION IMPLEMENTATION	SOLUTION ASSESSMENT
BRAINSTORMING - BRAINWRITING Team members discuss ideas on the issue. Brainwriting is like Brainstorming only people write their ideas down on paper and the paper is collected at the end of the session and the ideas are listed on a flip chart.	X	X					
FLOW CHARTS	X	X	X		X	X	X
CHECKSHEETS			X		X	X	
PARETO DIAGRAMS		X		X			X
CAUSE & EFFECT DIAGRAM		X	X		X		

TQM Basic Tools Matrix

TOOLS:	PROBLEM DEFINITION	PROBLEM ANALYSIS	DATA COLLECTION	DATA ANALYSIS	SOLUTION DEVELOPMENT	SOLUTION IMPLEMENTATION	SOLUTION ASSESSMENT
GRAPHS	X	X		X			X
CONTROL CHART		X		X			X
HISTOGRAM		X		X			X
SCATTER DIAGRAM		X		X			X
TIMELINES		X	X		X		

TQM Basic Tools Matrix

TOOLS:	PROBLEM DEFINITION	PROBLEM ANALYSIS	DATA COLLECTION	DATA ANALYSIS	SOLUTION DEVELOPMENT	SOLUTION IMPLEMENTATION	SOLUTION ASSESSMENT
FORCE FIELD ANALYSIS Supporting Opposing Culture — Tradition Society — Fear Work — Control Market —		X			X		
AFFINITY DIAGRAM Barriers Facilitators • Finances • Training • Knowledge • Support • Time • Teams						X	X
PROCESS MODELING INPUT PROCESS OUTPUT	X	X			X	X	X

TQM Basic Tools Matrix

FLOWCHART

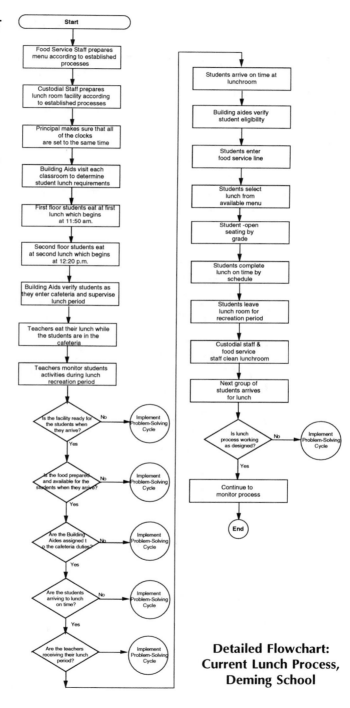

**Detailed Flowchart:
Current Lunch Process,
Deming School**

The preceding diagram is an example of a **detailed flowchart**. A flowchart is a diagram of the steps in a process. Using flowcharts prevents the team from leap-frogging over activities which are a natural sequence in the process. By showing how the process works, the team can identify potential problem areas and create a new and improved process. It is useful to create a flowchart as part of the process of thinking through a new process before it is implemented so that potential problems can be avoided.

In the preceding example, the team used this detailed flowchart to diagram the sequence for the school lunch process. This chart shows all of the stages that must be followed during the school lunch process. Two frequently asked questons are "How complicated does the flow-

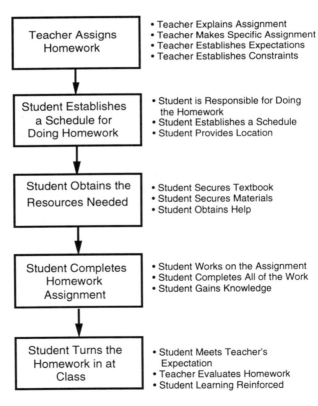

Top-Down Flowchart

chart have to be?" and "Are there standard international symbols to use when developing a flowchart?" The flowchart can be as simple or as complicated as you want it to be. Your knowledge of the problem area will determine how complex you make the flowchart. One of the tools used to develop a flowchart is **brainstorming**. In brainstorming, the group lists the steps in the process and puts them in sequential order.

There are no international standards specific to the symbols used in flowcharts. Computer programmers use flowcharts to depict how their computer applications run. The symbols in the flowcharts in this chapter are those used to develop computer flowcharts. A diamond represents a decision, a circle represents the end of a process, and a rectangle represents a function.

Another type of flowchart is the **top-down flowchart** (depicted on the previous page). The top-down flowchart is easy to use, and students generally find that it is a great tool to use to plan their homework activities.

CHECK SHEET

ITEM	GROUP A	GROUP B	GROUP C	GROUP D	GROUP E	GROUP F	GROUP G

The check sheet is an excellence tool for recording data. In the extreme left-hand column, the items against which the groups will be assessed are listed. Generally, a check mark indicates that the task is completed or that the item is secured. This is a very simple and quick way to keep track of students, books, or supplies. The attendance sheet in school is an example of a check sheet.

PARETO DIAGRAM

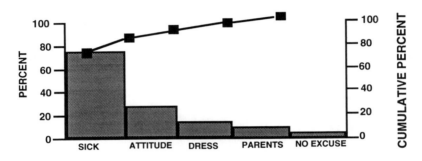

REASONS FOR STUDENT ABSENCES

A Pareto chart is a simple tool that helps to focus efforts on the problems that offer the greatest potential for improvement. By focusing everyone's efforts on one or two major components of a problem, it becomes easier to make progress. The basic structure of a Pareto chart is the same as a histogram. The Pareto chart can be used effectively to establish priorities.

In the example above, the Pareto chart was used by a teacher–student team to study the reasons for excessive student absences from class. The team found that the vast majority of absences were due to illness. Therefore, they directed their attention toward instituting a student health-care program that focused on illness prevention. The end result was a dramatic decrease in the number of students who were absent from class due to illness.

CAUSE-AND-EFFECT DIAGRAM (FISHBONE DIAGRAM)

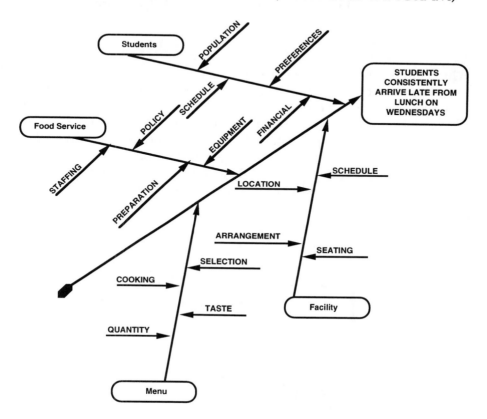

The cause-and-effect diagram, or fishbone diagram, is helpful in determining the root causes and effects within a school or district's processes and systems. It can be used to identify the components in the process that are responsible for an existing problem. The cause-and-effect diagram can be used to plan new processes more effectively and efficiently. This helps to ensure that the program meets the customer's requirements the first time.

As a tool, the cause-and-effect diagram is used to analyze a problem. The problem the team wants to study is described in the large box at the head of the arrow. In the example above, the team at a high school wants to eliminate the problems that are causing students to consistently arrive late from lunch on Wednesdays. On the main bones of the fish, the team listed the major factors that might contribute to the outcome. The team determined that the facility, menu, food service, and students were possible major factors. On the little bones, the team listed the factors that could possibly contribute to the major factors which ultimately led to the current outcome. After reviewing this process, the team determined that the policy established by the principal was responsible for the problem. The students had complained to the principal that the hamburgers they received on Wednesdays were always served cold. The principal had instructed the food service staff to cook the burgers ahead of time. This change in policy resulted in an outcome that was unacceptable to the students. To eliminate this problem, the school purchased food warmers to keep the hamburgers at an acceptable temperature.

GRAPH

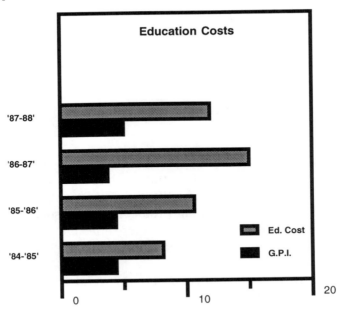

A graph is a simple tool to use. It is easy to understand and provides a visual comparison. The example above is a graph that compares the increase in the Gross Price Index (G.P.I.) to the total increase in educa-tion spending from 1984 to 1988. The vertical axis is the dollar measure-ment, and the horizontal axis is the time measurement. The graph illus-trates that the growth in the cost of education has significantly exceeded the growth in the G.P.I. The G.P.I. reflects the effect of inflation and price increase on the cost of consumer goods and services.

CONTROL CHART

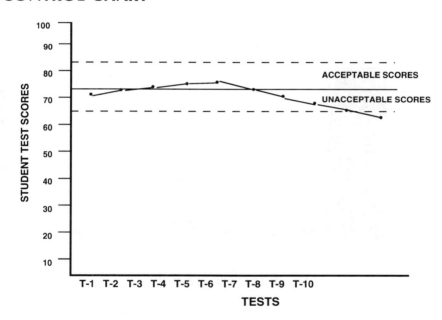

The control chart is used to graphically display the variation in an on-going process. The horizontal axis is used to track time, and the vertical axis is used to track the process under review. If the process goes out-side the lower control limits, it is considered to be "out of statistical control." This is a warning that the system needs to be adjusted or brought back into control.

The control chart in the example above was used by students to track their test scores. The students established 75 points as their point of reference. Test scores that went below the solid line (75 points) indi-cated that the students did not understand the material and that extra attention was needed in these areas. In this case, exceeding the upper limit was considered good; although it is technically out of statistical control, it is acceptable in this case.

HISTOGRAM

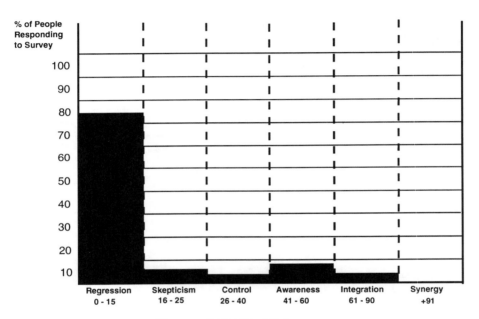

Phases of Quality Histogram

A histogram is a bar chart representation of the spread or dispersion of data. A Phases of Quality histogram graphically illustrates the Phase of Quality in a school or district. The histogram above shows the Phase of Quality for the administrators and teachers in a district.

SCATTER DIAGRAM

A scatter diagram is used to study the possible relationship between one variable and another. Occasionally, scatter diagrams are used to

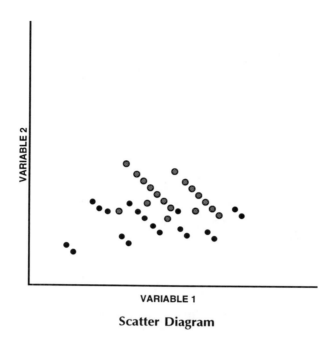

VARIABLE 1

Scatter Diagram

test for possible cause-and-effect relationships. A scatter diagram is created by setting up the horizontal axis to represent the measurement of value of one variable. The vertical axis represent the measurement of the second variable. (A word of caution: Scatter diagrams should be used only for comparison of fifty or more paired variables. Data comparisons of less than fifty or more paired variables are of little, if any, value. In fact, scatter diagrams are rarely used in implementing TQM in education.)

TIMELINE CHART

A timeline chart is an excellent project management tool. It is used to track assignments and develop milestones against which progress can be measured. Although computer-based project management systems are available, it is not necessary to get that technical. Basic timeline charts are easy to construct and simple to use. Students use them to

INDIVIDUAL	TASK	PROJECT DURATION								
JOHNSON	Flow Chart Admissions Process									
SMITH	Survey Students									
PHILLIPS	Examine Other Admission Systems									

Timeline Chart

track their progress in completing school projects. In the example above, Johnson is going to develop a flowchart of the school's central admissions process. The team has determined that Johnson will need approximately two weeks to complete the task. The team has assigned Smith the task of surveying students, and that task is projected to take approximately one and one-half weeks. The timeline chart enables the team to establish project milestones and objectives. It is an effective tool for keeping the team focused and on track.

FORCE FIELD ANALYSIS

Force field analysis is used to identify the factors opposing change and those pushing for change. By weighing the factors on both sides, a plan can be developed to effectively counterbalance the negative factors. Use of this tool helps to ensure the success of every quality project. In the example on the next page, a local high school has developed a force field analysis for adopting quality in schools. The students listed the driving forces that are demanding more from education and those forces that are opposing any change in the system. The major

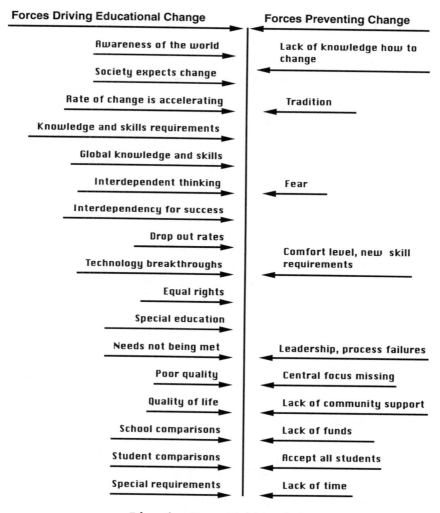

Forces Driving Educational Change

Awareness of the world

Society expects change

Rate of change is accelerating

Knowledge and skills requirements

Global knowledge and skills

Interdependent thinking

Interdependency for success

Drop out rates

Technology breakthroughs

Equal rights

Special education

Needs not being met

Poor quality

Quality of life

School comparisons

Student comparisons

Special requirements

Forces Preventing Change

Lack of knowledge how to change

Tradition

Fear

Comfort level, new skill requirements

Leadership, process failures

Central focus missing

Lack of community support

Lack of funds

Accept all students

Lack of time

Education Force Field Analysis

force opposing change is fear. When developing a quality culture, a support system must be developed for those individuals who are opposed to change. Once these individuals understand what quality in education really means, they become the strongest proponents of the program.

AFFINITY DIAGRAM

Facilitators	Barriers
• Cannot Afford not to Do Better • Helps You to do Your Job Better • Training Available • Cultural Transformation Required • Applies Equally to all Schools	• Finances • Time • Lack of Understanding • Cynicism: Just Another Program • Business Application

An affinity diagram is a simple process that is used to categorize elements of a process that have a natural link with one another. It is similar to a force field analysis. The affinity diagram is used to develop the cause-and-effect diagram and to evaluate the force field analysis. The affinity diagram and force field analysis are both simple to use. In each instance, the barriers or opposing forces are listed on one side and the positive or moving forces are listed on the other side. Both tools are extremely valuable in developing an implementation plan. They enable you to anticipate conflict. Once you know the areas where conflict is most likely to arise, you can develop a plan to minimize or eliminate the causes of conflict.

PROCESS MODELING

Process modeling is sometimes called functional modeling. It depicts the actual work process. Process modeling is used to analyze complex processes. In the example on the following page, the teacher developed a process model of the student services organization for a school in England. This approach enabled the teacher to understand the natural progression in the work flow for a new student entering the college. A process model is an effective tool for identifying the customer/supplier chain. It enables you to determine your customer's requirements and translate them into supplier specifications. Process modeling is also an effective tool for measuring the cost of quality. It allows a complex process to be divided into smaller processes that can be evaluated and measured.

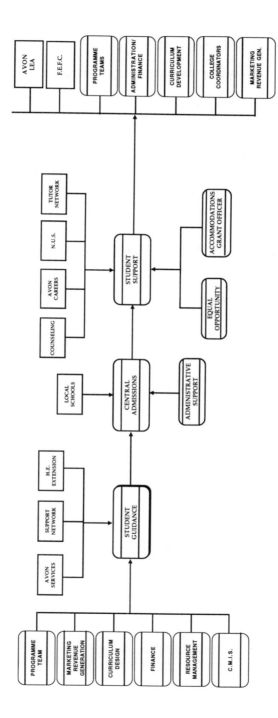

Process Modeling: Functional Overview of Student Services

PROFESSIONAL ASSESSMENT

Professional Development Assessment Process

A training assessment is a comparison between a normative criterion (*what should be*) and the condition of the group or individual being audited (*what is*). We tend to assume that all is well until the facts show otherwise. When TQM fails, the lack of training provided to individuals or groups who are expected to implement the concepts and procedures is usually the major contributing factor. Their "people skills" have not been properly developed.

Steps in the Professional Development Assessment Process

The training assessment process outlined below is comprehensive in scope and designed to recognize an organization's relationship to its environment. It also identifies the relationships that exist between the district or school and its parts. Achievement is compared to stated goals in a non-threatening, non-blaming manner. Present conditions (*what is*) are compared with desirable criteria (*what should be*). Education professionals will do what is best for the system if the facts are sound.

Step 1. Interview current staff and their administrators to find out exactly what it is that the managers and people in a particular function do. Focus on the major tasks, responsibilities, knowledge, and skill requirements of the job. Next, analyze all the data and turn it into behaviorally oriented job competencies. Each should represent a separate knowledge, skill, or ability that a person needs to perform well in the job. Prepare a list of competencies.

Step 2. Use the competency statements to describe each individual job. Give the statements to each person, along with instructions on how to profile his or her job. Each person needs to judge every competency statement according to how important it is to performing the job successfully.

Step 3. You now have profiles that describe the relative importance of each skill for successful job performance. However, they do not describe the degree of competence that is needed for "quality" performance. To identify the required skill level, ask the individuals to rate the proficiency levels required for each competency. Use the answers to prepare overall proficiency levels.

Step 4. Use the competencies to identify the strengths and weaknesses of each person. Give the complete list of job profile competencies to each individual, supplier, supervisor, peer, and customer who works with the person. These people will each have a different perspective on the skill requirements. You can now rank skill competencies.

Step 5. You can now evaluate the individual's proficiency in each competency. With this information, it is relatively simple to identify the specific training requirements for the individual. Simply compare the person's mastery of the specific competencies with the degree of mastery required for the job.

Step 6. This model is also useful for preparing individual career plans. The strengths and weakness of particular individuals can be determined. The overall information can be used to develop an individual professional development program for each person in the district or school.

Sample Professional Development Assessment Questionnaire

The questionnaire on the following page is designed to measure TQM proficiency. Once levels of proficiency have been determined, the team can develop individual professional development plans. This facilitates the change process that must occur in order for the school or district to develop a TQM focus.

TQM Tools Used in the Professional Development Assessment Process

The TQM tools discussed in the preceding sections are used to develop the Professional Development Assessment model. Special emphasis is placed on developing good listening skills. Additionally, the use of con-

Supervision

1. How long have you worked in your organization? _____

2. How long have you supervised the staff? _____

3. How long have you been the supervisor of your group? _____

4. How many staff do you supervise? _____

5. How many staff are you budgeted for? _____

Management

1. How many staff did you hire this past year? _____

2. How many staff did you release this past year? _____

3. How do you train your new staff:

a. Formal training program _____

b. Informal training program _____

c. Written training routine _____

d. Training staff _____

e. On-the-job training _____

4. How many staff did you conduct performance reviews for during the past year? _____

5. How often does your staff receive training:

a. Never _____

b. As needed _____

c. Formal program _____

d. When requested _____

Group Dynamics

(Answer yes or no to the following)

1. The group regularly plans activities. _____

2. We are experienced in problem-solving techniques. _____

3. We establish priorities for all of our projects. _____

4. The group is motivated to seek new ways of doing things. _____

5. As a result of training we have improved efficiency. _____

6. Natural leaders tend to surface in the project teams. _____

7. All of the teams pay attention to details. _____

8. Control is not an issue in the group. _____

9. The project teams are flexible and support each other's activities. _____

10. All of our projects support the group's goals and objectives. _____

11. Communication is important to our success. _____

12. Members of the group are encouraged to take risks. _____

13. We manage and anticipate conflict. _____

14. The group develops strategic plans. _____

15. We develop a systems perspective for all our processes. _____

16. Everyone participates in the project teams. _____

17. Everyone is aware of all of the groups projects and activities. _____

18. We can measure the results of our improvement teams. _____

Professional Development Assessment Questionnaire

Individuals

Item								Percent Below Level
Organizing & Planning								
Problem Solving								
Priority Setting								
Motivation								
Efficiency								
Selection								
Leadership								
Knowledge of User Support								
Attention to Detail								
Control								
Flexibility								
Goal Orientation								
Oral Communication								
Risk Taking								
Strategic Thinking								
System Perspective								
Decisiveness								
Conflict Resolution								
Team Participation								
Written Communication								

Key: △ High Discrepancy   ○ Moderate Discrepancy   ✗ Low Discrepancy

**Total Quality Management Professional Development Requirements
(By Required Proficiency Level)**

flict management is extensive in the development of the Professional Development Assessment process. Specifically, the following tools are utilized:

- Brainstorming
- Brainwriting
- Check sheets
- Interviewing
- Surveying
- Conflict management

SUMMARY

In this chapter, the basic problem-solving tools of quality were reviewed. The review began with an analysis of the quality process for building effective quality teams. This process was recently used in the County of Avon, Bristol, England to provide the county's educational advisors with training in the use and application of TQM tools and techniques. The director of education commented that he had never seen the group work as a team before. He did not believe that the training would be as effective as it was.

The review moved to a discussion of the ways in which TQM tools are used to analyze and solve problems. An overview of the basic tools of quality was provided. Application of these tools will enable you to improve the quality of every educational process in your school or district. Once you master the use of these tools, you can expand your TQM tool usage to include the advanced statistical process control tools.

The review concluded by examining ways to assess the professional development of management and staff. As stated in an earlier chapter, TQM begins and ends with training. The system developed here will enable you to assess your staff's strengths and weaknesses and to design a quality training program to provide them with the skills to implement quality.

CHAPTER 13

COST OF QUALITY

In previous chapters, we explored what quality means and why it is important for education to adopt a quality philosophy. In this chapter, we will discover the true costs of not doing quality work. Oftentimes, this is a difficult concept for educators to grasp. Many education professionals who were interviewed prior to developing quality programs believed that there was no cost associated with poor quality in education. Unfortunately, any time the wrong things are done right or the right things are done wrong, there are costs to the educational system. These costs include wasted resources, lost opportunities to influence students, poor use of budget dollars, job dissatisfaction, student disinterest, and lack of community support.

Every project will result in either direct or indirect cost savings. **Direct cost savings are the savings in real dollars.** Direct cost savings are "hard" measurable dollars. For example, a teacher who spends $300 on copying material for her class and then implements a process change that reduces the cost to $250 has achieved a direct cost saving. It can be measured and is reflected in the budget.

People tend to overlook indirect cost savings. Indirect cost savings are more difficult to measure but are just as important as direct cost savings. **Indirect cost savings are the "soft" dollar savings realized from a system or process change.** For example, it initially took two staff members three hours each to process the payroll. A system change eliminated one person from the process. There were no direct cost savings because the second person is now working on other tasks. There are, however, indirect savings for the district (one person's salary for three hours). The indirect cost savings help the school or district to become more productive.

The Quality Initiative Cost Savings Graph depicted below is used to document the total direct and indirect cost savings realized by the district. Only the total dollar savings are shown on the graph. Projects are

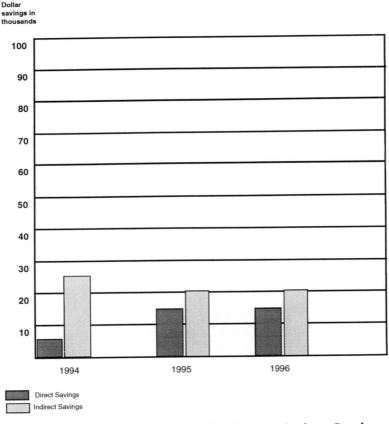

District-Wide 5 + 5 Quality Initiative Cost Savings Graph

not listed, individuals participating on the project team are not identified, and departments are not recognized for their contributions.

In this example, the district decided to track the cost savings for a three-year period. Generally, savings realized in the initial year of a project will provide the district with cost benefits in subsequent years. It is not necessary to project future cost savings for the district. However, it is necessary to depict the current cost savings. The graph clearly demonstrates the financial benefits of the quality initiative for a school or district.

QUALITY APPLICATION GRID

Quality cannot be applied to everyone's work processes. Work can be divided into four quadrants: (1) must do, (2) priority, (3) like to do and necessary, and (4) like to do and not necessary. The Quality Application Grid on the following page was developed for Soundwell College in Bristol, England. To which quadrant can quality be applied?

This system places work into one of the four quadrants and determines the amount of resources that are required to complete each task. Educational resources are not unlimited. Therefore, it is important to be very careful in assigning the right resources to the right tasks. If too many resources or the wrong resources are assigned to a task, resources are being wasted. These are avoidable costs. Use of the Quality Application Grid minimizes avoidable costs.

In which quadrant does quality work? Quality will **only** work in the *priority* quadrant. It cannot be used in the other quadrants. Any attempt to apply quality principles to the tasks in the other quadrants will fail.

Quality will not work in the *must do* quadrant because time is not available to plan for or implement quality. The tasks in the *must do* quadrant must be completed as quickly as possible. Constraints are imposed on the tasks in this quadrant. For example, one school district was planning a major training event for the district staff during the first week of the new school term. The district training team committed themselves to this task in January. Two weeks prior to the training event, the team began to work on the training program. They were facing a deadline that was the driving force. Quality was not an issue—getting the task done was the issue.

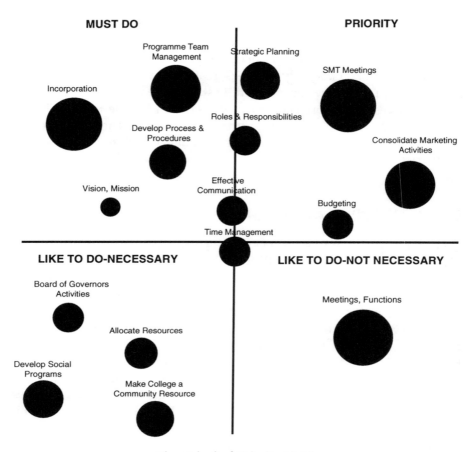

MUST DO

Programme Team
Management

Strategic Planning

SMT Meetings

Incorporation

Roles & Responsibilities

Develop Process &
Procedures

Consolidate Marketing
Activities

Vision, Mission

Effective
Communication

Budgeting

Time Management

PRIORITY

LIKE TO DO-NECESSARY

Board of Governors
Activities

Allocate Resources

Develop Social
Programs

Make College a
Community Resource

LIKE TO DO-NOT NECESSARY

Meetings, Functions

Vice-Principal Priority Matrix

Quality will work in the *priority* quadrant because time is available to plan for quality and properly use all of the tools of quality. In the example above, if the team had begun to plan for the training event in January, they could have developed a quality schedule for creating the training program. As it was, the event was a total waste of money and effort. We can, however, move a task from the *priority* quadrant to the *must do* quadrant. We move tasks from one quadrant to the other by our inaction. In January, the training event was a *priority* task which could be planned. In August, it became a *must do* task which could not adequately be planned.

Quality will not work in the other two quadrants because the tasks in those quadrants are things we like to do. Generally, when we take pleasure in doing a task, we exert the effort necessary to ensure that the task is done to our satisfaction. Unfortunately, we may waste effort in completing the task to our specifications. In fact, many items placed in the last two quadrants are tasks that can be assigned to another individual. For example, the vice-principal at one high school was spending approximately twenty hours a week managing the bus schedule. When asked why he spent so much time on the task, he stated that he found it a very rewarding and challenging task. Unfortunately, the rest of his work was not adequately done, and the superintendent of schools decided to assign the task to the director of transportation.

APPLYING YOUR KNOWLEDGE: EXERCISE

Map your work tasks in the quadrants below.

MUST DO	PRIORITY
LIKE TO DO-NECESSARY	**LIKE TO DO-NOT NECESSARY**

NECESSARY AND AVOIDABLE COSTS

There are two types of quality costs: necessary costs and avoidable costs. Necessary costs are required to achieve and sustain a defined standard of work. Quality training is a necessary cost. Avoidable costs occur whenever wrong things are done or things are done wrong. The example of the vice-principal managing the student bus transportation schedule is an example of an avoidable cost.

Necessary costs include prevention and inspection. Avoidable costs include some inspection costs and all failure costs.

Prevention costs are the costs of any actions that are intended to make sure that things will not go wrong. Inspection costs are the costs of finding out if and when things are going wrong so that corrective or preventive action can be taken. Region 3 Technical High School in Lincoln, Maine contacted recent graduates and employers in the area to determine the added value of the school's program. The costs associated with this program are prevention costs. The school's goal was to find out what did not work and fix it before it became a bigger problem. Failure costs are the costs incurred when a customer is or will be dissatisfied. Graduates from Region 3 Technical High School who cannot find jobs because the employers in the area believe that the graduates received a poor education are examples of failure costs for both the students and the school.

APPLYING YOUR KNOWLEDGE: EXERCISE

Identifying the necessary and avoidable costs of quality is the first step toward reducing those costs. Administrators and teachers are usually close enough to the situation to know where the waste really is. In this exercise, draw on your work experience to identify necessary and avoidable costs. In the process, you will also identify the prevention, inspection, and failure costs for your task.

Use the worksheet on the next page to record your answers.

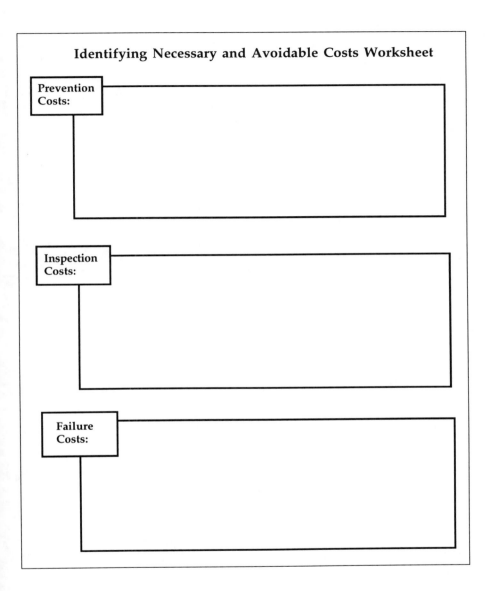

Identifying Necessary and Avoidable Costs Worksheet

Prevention
Costs:

Inspection
Costs:

Failure
Costs:

CHAPTER 14

CONTINUOUS IMPROVEMENT

Continuous improvement enables us to monitor our work processes in order to identify opportunities for improvement. The basic problem-solving tools reviewed in Chapter 12, such as the flowchart and the control chart, can be used to help build a successful customer/supplier partnership. With these tools, work processes can be continuously evaluated and improved in order to make the partnership work.

In a Total Quality School:

- There is room for improvement in every educational process.

- Every improvement, however big or small, is worthwhile.

- Small improvements add up to significant change.

- Mistakes are treated as opportunities to improve.

- Everyone shares responsibility for trying to prevent problems and for fixing problems when they do occur.

- Everyone in the school or district is committed to continuous improvement.

EXAMINING PROCESSES

As discussed in Chapter 10 on problem solving, a process is the work that is done to produce the service or product that is delivered to the customer. It is important to understand what you need in the way of inputs in order to carry out your process. Inputs can be materials, information, guidance, regulations, or court actions. It is also important to understand how your process adds value to the inputs you receive so that you can produce a quality output for your customer. Consider the added value of completing a student guidance report for submission to a college:

Inputs + Value-Added Process = Quality Outputs

This formula can also be viewed in terms of the customer/supplier chain. Your supplier gives you inputs. You add value to the inputs through your work process and convert and deliver these inputs as outputs to your customer. You are both customer (of inputs) and supplier (of outputs).

As discussed in Chapter 10, before you can begin to improve the overall flow of your work, you must first understand how your work processes fit together. By using a flowchart to examine the sequence of your work, you can locate bottlenecks and specific points where problems occur.

It is also important to take a close look at each process that is part of the work flow. The input–output model is like a zoom lens that focuses on and enlarges a process so that it can be closely examined. You must know just what goes on in each process, what the inputs are, and how value is added to them.

EXERCISE

Using the information in Chapter 10 on problem solving, develop a flowchart for the production of a school yearbook. Use the space on the following page to develop your flowchart.

Key Points

Flowcharts should:

- Represent all parts of the work
- Represent processes
- Represent the detailed steps in the work flow
- Be used to make changes
- Not be made without talking to all the stakeholders

INPUT–OUTPUT MODEL

An input–output model is a comprehensive list of what is needed to meet a specific customer requirement. It enlarges a particular process that is part of the overall work flow detailed on a flowchart. The model is used to help analyze the differences between the current state and the desired state that will meet the customer's requirements.

In Chapter 10, we discussed how to develop a process model. The following is an example of an input–output model:

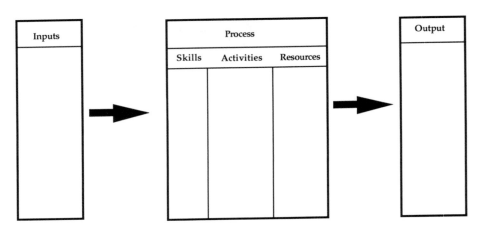

Step 1: Identify a specific output.

Step 2: List the knowledge, skills, activities, and resources needed to provide the output.

Step 3: List the inputs needed to do the work.

It is important to know how well a process is performing in order to:

- Ensure that it is capable of meeting customer requirements

- Correct process problems before they affect the output

- Improve the process to meet changing customer needs

The performance of a process varies from day to day. Some minor variation is normal and is the result of causes that cannot be easily controlled or changed (i.e., winter conditions); however, other variations that exceed normal limits are the result of problems or influences that can be controlled.

Random, uncontrollable variations that affect a process are called *common causes*; if only common causes are at work, the process is in control. Common causes result from many factors, each of which may affect the process to a small degree. Common causes are often due to design and operating limitations, and it may be impractical or difficult to remove them from the process. In fact, the slight, daily variation that is due to common causes usually has only a minimal effect on the overall process.

On the other hand, a process that exceeds certain statistically determined operating limits is out of control. Action must be taken quickly to determine the specific cause of the variation and correct it. If *special causes* are at work, the process is out of control. Unlike common causes, special causes:

- Have a significant effect on a process

- Affect a process in unpredictable ways

- Provide immediate opportunities for improving process performance

A control chart can be used to show how a process is functioning. (See the discussion of control charts in Chapter 12.) It enables you to:

- Determine whether your process is in or out of control

- Detect trends in process performance that indicate the effect of a special cause

- Evaluate the overall effect of common causes on process variation to decide whether a process should be overhauled or redesigned

Creating a Control Chart

Step 1: Select a variable that is a good indicator of performance of the process.

Step 2: Choose a way to measure the variable selected.

Step 3: Select time intervals at which measurements should be made.

Step 4: Create a chart for the aspect of the process that will be measured over time. Label the vertical axis with the units of measure for the variable. Label the horizontal axis with the units of time over which the variable will be measured.

Step 5: Determine the range for the process (i.e., upper and lower control limits).

Step 6: Enter measurements on the chart. Monitor the chart for changes that may indicate whether the process is out of control.

CONTINUOUS IMPROVEMENT

Continuous improvement is central to any quality organization. It can only be achieved when everyone in the school or district is working together and

- Applies the quality wheel to every aspect of work

- Understands the long-term advantage of a cost-of-quality approach

- Encourages all improvements, both big and small

- Focuses on prevention instead of fighting fires

The commitment of Total Quality Schools to continuous improvement will usually result in *kaizen* and/or breakthrough improvement. *Kaizen* focuses on small steady improvements. *Kaizen* and breakthrough are essentially the two major categories of improvement.

Kaizen is a Japanese term that means improving work through a series of small, gradual, ongoing changes. Its also means setting standards that are within reach. A breakthrough is a dramatic improvement in work processes. It can occur in technology, in the way work is organized, or in the way people think. Although breakthroughs are important, they do not happen all the time. Improvement most often is the result of small continuous changes.

WHY TECHNIQUE

The Why Technique is a simple but effective way to move through the layers of causes in order to uncover the preventable root cause of a recurring problem. It is used to help find the root cause of a problem. The technique begins by asking why a problem occurs and then repeatedly asking why that problem happened until the most important cause is uncovered.

How to Use the Why Technique

Step 1: Select a recurring problem.

Step 2: Ask "Why did the problem occur?" to uncover the first-layer causes.

Step 3: Take the causes uncovered in Step 2 and ask "Why did they happen?" to uncover the second-layer causes.

Step 4: Continue asking why the previous causes happened until the most important root cause is uncovered.

The Why Technique can be used to uncover a number of causes at each level.

BENCHMARKING

Benchmarking is a structured process for gaining new perspectives on customer needs. The objective in benchmarking is to gain a competitive advantage by identifying, measuring, and emulating *best practices* both inside and outside your school or district. Benchmarking allows you to:

- Take a fresh look at standard practices

- Identify goals of excellence

- Facilitate *kaizen* and breakthrough process improvement

How to Use Benchmarking

Step 1: Identify the process to be improved.

Step 2: Identify the groups or organizations that perform this process very well.

Step 3: Measure to determine which organizations perform the process the best and what their level of performance is. This becomes the benchmark standard to meet and exceed.

Step 4: Study the methods of these other groups to find out how they perform the process so well.

Step 5: Apply these methods, with suitable alteration, to your own work processes.

SUMMARY

The following list is a recap of some of the key points in this chapter:

- A flowchart is used to describe the current sequence of activities and decision points in a process.

- A control chart is used to determine how a process is performing, before problems affect the output.

- Continuous improvement means that everyone shares responsibility for fixing and preventing problems; it also means striving for slow, steady improvement as well as breakthrough improvement.

- The Why Technique is used to uncover the root causes of problems.

- Benchmarking is used to help set improvement targets.

CHAPTER 15

CONCLUSION

Quality is hard work. It requires a commitment to excellence, a dedication to leadership, and a willingness to change. More often than not, you will encounter people who talk about the quality philosophy but do not follow the principles of quality. Quality should be the normal way in which people interact with one another.

Our schools are under constant pressure to change. In many instances, change is being forced upon schools by external forces. Business is prescribing its own solution for solving today's problems in education. Society is telling educators to do more with less. Professional educational associations are telling administrators and society how to improve the quality of education. Many of our nation's leading educational reform groups are criticizing educators for their resistance to change. These are only some of the issues impacting our education systems. If the quality of education is to improve, this constant flow of conflict must stop.

Education, business, and government professionals must learn to work together. Society must recognize that our nation's future success is dependent upon everyone working together to solve common problems. The problems impacting education were not created overnight and they cannot be solved quickly. The education environment is very complex. As indicated by the vast number of educational reform programs implemented in the past, a quick-fix solution is not the answer. Because of the complexity of the education environment, effective educational reform must be a systematic process.

Quality provides education professionals with the structure and techniques necessary to improve every educational process. Quality programs have been successfully implemented in hundreds of schools in America and England. Success has not been without pain, frustration, and challenge, however.

Change agents are not well received in any organization. Change is fearful for many people. As a quality leader, you will be asking people to change the way they work. Teachers will no longer be able to close the door and maintain a teacher-centered classroom. Administrators will be asked to include teachers and staff in the decision-making process. Support staff will be asked to work with teachers and administrators to develop new systems for creating quality educational support services.

Change, no matter how small, will not come easily. For example, the superintendent in one school district asked the teachers not to tape anything to the walls. Some of the teachers had created very elaborate themes for their rooms. However, in creating these "theme" environments, the teachers nailed, taped, stapled, and glued things to the walls. At the end of the year or whenever a teacher wanted to change the theme, support staff had to repair and repaint the walls. If the support staff could not complete the repairs according to the teacher's schedule, the teacher became indignant and demanded service. To resolve this problem, the superintendent and school board established a policy prohibiting the teachers from affixing anything to the walls.

The teachers did not react to this new policy in a quality manner. They became indignant. They felt that the classroom was their own environment. What went on in the classroom was the teacher's business and no one else's. Some of the teachers completely ignored the policy. They continued to do what they had done, and the district continued to encounter the same problems. Rather than enforce the policy, the superintendent and school board rescinded it.

What message does this send to the teachers and staff? If you are going to be a change agent, you must be able to withstand the challenges to change. Your commitment to change must be unwavering. As the quality leader, you must lead by example. As illustrated throughout this handbook, if you work hard, you will realize the benefits of quality—an improvement in every educational process from managing the classroom to maintaining the buildings.

INDEX